35

take five

D1375927

6/05

take five
rose elliot

CASSELL&co

First published in the United Kingdom
in 2001 by Cassell & Co

A CIP catalogue record for this book is available from the British Library.

ISBN 0304 354236

Designed by Miranda Harvey
Printed and bound in China

Cassell & Co
Wellington House
125 Strand
London WC2R 0BB

contents

introduction

Fruit and vegetables are good for us – that is common knowledge. Many studies have shown that we can dramatically improve our health by eating at least five portions of fruit and veg every day.

People who eat this amount, or more, have better resistance to disease, fewer problems with weight, less constipation, improved protection against heart disease and diabetes. And as for cancer, the benefits are very specific:

eating the recommended five portions of fruit and veg each day can reduce cancer rates by more than 20 per cent;

eating the recommended fruit and veg, staying physically active and maintaining a healthy weight can cut cancer risk by 30–40 per cent;

doing all the above and not smoking can cut cancer risk by 60–70 per cent.

If eating this amount of fruit and veg seems daunting, take heart. Once you get down to it, it's not that difficult. There are lots of wonderful ways to prepare and eat fruit and vegetables throughout the day, from breakfast mueslis to mid-morning juices and shakes; from lunchtime soups and sandwiches to lively supper and pudding ideas. Starters, salads and accompanying veg and even some cakes can all add positive variety to your diet.

But which fruit and vegetables should be used? Are they all equally good? And what size portions should you consume? All fruit and vegetables count except for potatoes. While being a healthy ingredient potatoes are classed as a starch and they need to be eaten in addition to the five portions of fruit and vegetables. A portion is probably the amount you'd be likely eat in one serving: for instance, a whole apple or pear; two good spoonfuls of greens; a shallow bowl of salad; or a glass of fruit juice.

Measured by weight, a portion is 80 g/3 oz and by eating five of these we reach the minimum 400 g/15 oz goal set by the World Health Organization. Eating two or three times that amount is even better. But most of us are only managing a measly two or three portions, or 150–250 g/6–9 oz each day.

balancing act

Eating more fruit and vegetables will naturally alter the balance of your diet. There will be less room for other foods, and if that means eating fewer sugary, salty and fatty foods, so much the better. But what about essential nutrients such as protein? Will eating more fruit and veg mean you'll go short of these?

The answer is no. Most of us are eating more protein than we really need. Replacing some of this with extra fruit and veg can only have a positive effect.

Fruit and veg contain over 100 beneficial vitamins, minerals and other substances, which interact with each other and with our body to keep us healthy. For instance, eating fresh fruit and vegetables with meals can help to prevent anaemia because the vitamin C in the fruit and veg increases our ability to absorb iron from meat, eggs, nuts, pulses and grains.

A healthy diet consists of some protein, generous amounts of starchy foods such as pasta, potatoes, rice, bread and couscous and, of course, five or more portions of fruit and veg.

how much?

An 80 g/3 oz portion is the sort of size most people would naturally serve, so you don't have to get your scales out at every meal time. Here are some examples:

Vegetables	Example	Portion
Green vegetables	broccoli, spinach	2 serving spoons
Root vegetables	carrots, parsnips	2 serving spoons
Small vegetables	peas, sweetcorn	3 serving spoons
Salad	lettuce, tomatoes, cucumber	1 dessert bowl

Fruit	Example	Portion
Large fruits	melon, pineapple	1 large slice
Medium fruits	apple, orange, banana	1 fruit
Small fruits	plum, kiwi, satsuma	2 fruits
Berry-type fruit	raspberries, strawberries, grapes	1 cupful
Fruit salad	stewed apple, canned peach slices	2–3 tablespoons
Dried fruits	apricots	1/2–1 serving spoon
Juice	orange, apple, carrot	1 medium glass (150 ml/5 fl oz)

Young children will need smaller portions and may not manage to eat five 80 g/3 oz portions every day. Encourage them to eat fruit and veg at every meal and to use them for snacks. That way they gain a healthy attitude to food early on.

fun with fruit, variety with veg

Five portions a day may sound like a lot, but when you try it, you'll find it's not really that difficult. If you think about what you're eating each day, the chances are you'll need to make only a few changes to bring your diet up to scratch.

If your fruit and vegetable intake is very low at the moment, you'll need to rethink your meals and snacks a little more, but it can be done. Try introducing an extra portion every day for a week and then continue with another the next week and so on until you're reaching your total. Use these examples as a guide:

Example 1

Time	Fruit or vegetable	Portions
Breakfast	Glass of apple or orange juice	1
	Cereal with chopped banana	1
	Toast	
Mid-morning	Apple or grapes	1
Lunch	Sandwiches	
	An apple	1
Evening meal	Slice of melon	1
	Pizza	
	Bowl of salad	1
Total number of portions of fruit and vegetables		6

Example 2

Time	Fruit or vegetable	Portions
Breakfast	Glass of apple or orange juice	1
	Cooked breakfast	
Lunch	Glass of apple or tomato juice	1
	Baked potato	
	Bowl of salad	1
Evening meal	Main dish with potatoes and	2
	two vegetables, eg carrots and peas	
	Apple pie or fruit salad	1
Total number of portions of fruit and vegetables		6

Both of these meal plans actually include six portions of fruit and veg and it would be quite easy to add even more with extra snacks of crudités, fresh fruit, a few raisins or another glass or fruit or vegetable juice.

Even if you don't really like cooking, there are plenty of ways you can enjoy fruit and vegetables. For instance:

juice for breakfast, or during the day instead of tea or coffee;
juice before a meal, as a starter – go for something exotic or pour a well-loved favourite such as tomato juice;
fresh fruit snacks – an apple, a banana, a handful of nuts and raisins;
ready-washed salad with a meal;
an additional vegetable with a meal – ready-to-cook or frozen vegetables make it easy;
fresh, ready-prepared or canned fruit for dessert.

buying and storing

Delicate fruits and most vegetables with the exception of potatoes, onions, sweet potatoes and squash, keep best in the refrigerator.

Organic fruit and vegetables make excellent sense from the health, flavour and ecological points of view and joining a 'box scheme' (a contract for regular delivery or collection) ensures a constant and varied supply of seasonal produce.

Wash all fruit and vegetables before use; it can be helpful to do this before you put them in the fridge so they're quick and easy to use.

Ready-prepared raw fruit and vegetables cost more, but can be a timesaving boon when you're tired and hurried.

Frozen fruit and vegetables can be very handy; raspberries, fruits of the forest, petit pois, sweetcorn, mixed casserole vegetables, spinach and broad beans are particularly useful.

Some canned fruit and vegetables such as tomatoes, sweetcorn, artichoke hearts, apricots and lychees make life easier too.

The variety of fruit and vegetables has never been so great and there are many fabulous ways to prepare, cook and eat them. So give it a try, and see how much better you feel.

veg made easy

With the variety of vegetables available throughout the year and the number of different yet simple ways to cook them, it must be possible to please even the most unenthusiastic vegetable eater. And for convenience, fresh ready-to-use or frozen vegetables make it practical to cook them even if you're too tired or too rushed to do the preparation.

There are a number of quick and easy methods for cooking vegetables. The following offer a wide range of possibilities.

Microwaving
So clean and easy, especially with ready-prepared vegetables in packets, this method is simplicity itself. Just make a couple of steam holes in the packet and microwave until the vegetables are done to suit your taste. The actual cooking time is not always a lot less, but it saves time not having to use a pan, boil the water and wash up afterwards. After cooking, open the packet carefully, protecting your hands and face from the steam.

You can also use this method for vegetables you have prepared yourself. Put them into a shallow microwavable container, add 2–3 tablespoons of water (except for spinach, which doesn't need it), cover with a plate or clingfilm punched with a few steam-holes and microwave.

Half boiling, half steaming
This is my favourite way of cooking any leafy green vegetable, apart from spinach, which doesn't need any additional water. For the rest, bring about 1 cm/½ inch of water to the boil and put in the vegetables, most of which will be above the water. Bring back to the boil, cover with a lid and let them boil until they are as tender as you like them.

Steaming
This method is good for vegetables that cook quickly, such as small florets of cauliflower or broccoli, slim French beans, mangetouts or sugar-snap peas, which take hardly any time at all.

The kind of steamer that fits over a saucepan is best because you can cook two different types of vegetable at the same time – one type boiling or half boiling-half steaming underneath and another in the steamer on top.

Boiling
For longer-cooking vegetables such as potatoes, carrots, swede or turnips, cover them with water in a saucepan, bring to the boil, cover the pan and boil gently until they're done.

For faster-cooking vegetables including French beans and halved Brussels sprouts, make sure the water is boiling before you put them in, boil uncovered and test often with the point of a knife or a skewer, so they don't become soggy and overcooked.

Stir-frying
Although this method is often associated with healthy eating, it can be rather high in fat unless you're careful.

Heat a tablespoonful or two of oil in a wok or large saucepan until hot and put in the vegetables, which need to be cut according to how long they take to cook: the faster the cooking, the larger the piece. Stir-fry, tossing and stirring frequently, over a high heat for a few minutes until the vegetables are done.

Grilling, roasting and baking
This is such a simple and delicious way to prepare veg. Simply place the vegetable on the grill pan or in a shallow roasting tin and brush with a little olive oil or a half-and-half mixture of olive oil and lemon juice, or spray with an oil and water mix made up in a spray bottle (4–5 parts water to 1 part olive oil).

Put the vegetables under a hot grill or into a hot oven. Some vegetables don't even need oil, for instance jacket potatoes, beetroots, onions baked in their skins, peppers, tomatoes and mushrooms, which soon produce all the liquid necessary.

Griddling
One of those frying pans with ridges in the bottom is great for cooking thin strips of vegetables such as aubergines and courgettes and flat pieces of pepper. You only need to brush them very lightly with oil, or oil and lemon juice. Cook them on one side until dark lines appear, flip them over with a spatula and do the other side.

Griddled vegetables taste great, but this isn't as practical as grilling or roasting because you can only do a few at a time and the kitchen can become filled with a smoky fog. It's better for cooking in advance or for just a couple of people.

great ideas

Fresh vegetables, perfectly cooked, need few extras when being served as an accompaniment to a main course. Just drain them and season with coarse sea salt that you can crush over them with your fingers and freshly ground pepper from a mill. However, you can always try some of the following simple ideas to add colour, flavour and texture to your vegetables:

- a squeeze of fresh lemon or lime juice (this really brings out the flavour);
- grated lemon or lime zest;
- chopped fresh herbs (experiment with different ones for variety);
- a splash of soy sauce;
- crushed garlic;
- butter, olive oil or toasted sesame oil (on vegetables cooked without fat or oil);
- a sprinkling of toasted sesame seeds, flaked almonds or pine nuts;
- freshly grated nutmeg;
- quirky additions like capers, pickled ginger, chopped stem ginger, pickled green peppercorns, sun-dried tomatoes snipped into shreds, crushed juniper berries.

Experiment and find your favourites!

the ultimate detox diet

One of the best ways to kick-start any fresh approach to your diet is by giving yourself a detox boost. My favourite cleansing diet is the tried and tested 'grape cure', which is safe and gentle. For best results you need to do it for at least three days because it takes that time for your body to realise that a cleansing is taking place. You can continue for five to six days, which some practitioners believe gives the optimum results, but don't continue for any longer than this without medical supervision.

Each day you need to take four or five meals of grapes. A meal consists of the amount of grapes you can hold in your two cupped hands; don't exceed this quantity. You can use red or white grapes but don't use seedless ones. Eat the grapes skin, pips and all, chewing them slowly and thoroughly.

It is important to drink at least 4 litres/7 pints of pure mineral water each day to wash away the toxins that the grapes will be releasing from your system. Also, take garlic tablets each day, following the directions on the bottle, to help the cleansing process.

You may feel more tired than usual while following this detox programme, so it's a good idea to do it at a time when you can be kind to yourself and rest when you need to.

After three to six days, ease yourself gently out of the diet by eating grapes for breakfast; a small bowl of vegetable soup, or a plate of cooked vegetables or salad for lunch; and an evening meal consisting of cooked vegetables and some light protein, such as tofu or fish, or some well-cooked brown rice.

just juice – a one-day detox plan

For a one-day detox, why not give your digestive system a complete rest and have just juice? Plan ahead so that you choose a day when you can relax at home: this is a day for *you*, so spoil yourself. Have a long, luxurious bath – as long as you don't suffer from high-blood pressure you could make this into a bit of a DIY sauna by adding a handful of epsom salts and wrapping up warm for several hours afterwards to allow your body to sweat out impurities.

You can choose the juices you fancy: you can stick to one type of fruit juice all day or have different ones. Have just 3–4 glasses at mealtimes, but you can go up to a maximum of 8, so write a shopping list and make sure you've got all your ingredients handy before you start. Begin with fruit or carrot juices in the morning and either continue with these all day or introduce some stronger vegetable juices. Try pure darling clementine (see page 107) or sunrise cocktail (see page 105) early in the day, followed by five-star ruby (see page 111), carrot with a ginger top (see page 111) or four-star top-up (see page 110).

If you haven't got a juicer, try cold-pressed organic juices from large supermarkets and health shops or, if you've got a blender, why not try some smoothies? For best results on a detox day, choose pure fruit mixtures (without milk, nuts or sweetenings) such as three-fruit smoothie (see page 105), watermelon ginger (see page 106), tropical smoothie (see page 107), pineapple and mango punch (see page 108) or strawberry orange delight (see page 108).

When you're not drinking juices, sip plenty of natural still mineral water or filtered water but don't have any tea, coffee or other drinks.

After this one-day detox you'll emerge feeling relaxed, energised, a little leaner and ready to face the world afresh.

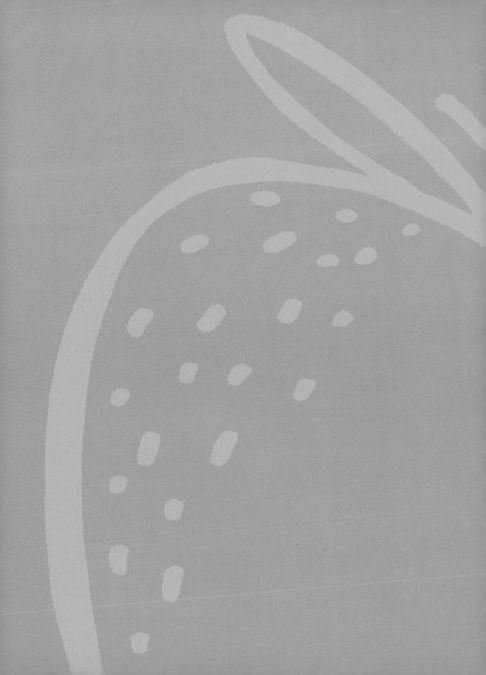

breakfast

quick ideas

Breakfast is a good time to eat at least one portion of fruit or vegetables. Fresh fruit juice is a natural choice at this time of day. So is fresh fruit. But why not have both? A glass of orange juice and half a sweet pink grapefruit make a refreshing start. Or try a wedge of juicy, fragrant melon, served cold from the fridge.

Strategies for including more fruit and vegetables on their own, with cereal, toast or a cooked breakfast follow, along with an array of recipes to start the day in new, healthier ways.

Fruit feast
Eat fresh fruit on its own: if you start the day with an apple, an orange and a banana, that's three portions without really trying! Buy a ripe mango, cut down each side of the shallow stone, peel and slice the flesh and enjoy.

When summer fruits are in season, savour a bowl of ripe cherries, strawberries, raspberries, apricots, or sliced peaches. Make a fruit salad, mixing fresh and dried fruit if desired.

Fruity cereal
Add some fresh fruit to breakfast cereal or muesli, such as chopped banana, chopped or grated sweet apple, chopped juicy pear, sweet strawberries or seedless grapes.

Try adding soaked or ready-to-eat dried apricots or prunes, or other dried fruits such as plump, sweet figs, dried peaches, dried pears, dried cherries or raisins. Serve hot porridge or creamy rice with sliced banana, fruit purée, apricot compote (see page 26) or a really fruity jam or fruit conserve.

Fruit yogurt

Add your own chopped fruit to plain yogurt and sweeten to taste with sugar or honey for luscious, ultra-fruity yogurt. For a special treat, add a big spoonful of fruit compote or fruit jam to plain yogurt, and toss in some chopped fresh fruit. Serve sliced peaches or other fresh fruit topped with thick yogurt and a dollop of raspberry or black cherry jam. Make creamy, frothy fruit shakes using yogurt.

Jump for juices

Breakfast is a great time to start the day with a juice and there are many sumptuous varieties. For a full selection of juices that can be used at breakfast or indeed any time of day, see page 104.

Topped toast

Top freshly made toast with mashed banana, sliced avocado, hot canned tomatoes, fried mushrooms, creamed sweetcorn, or cooked asparagus. Or give a special flourish to hot toast with tomato slices, sprinkled with grated cheese and grilled for a few minutes until the tomato is hot and lightly cooked and the cheese melted and golden brown. A thick, generous layer of a really fruity conserve spread on toast is a great way to top up your fruit quota.

Breakfast bonanza

If you're having a cooked breakfast, start with fruit juice and/or fruit. Add some vegetables, such as grilled tomatoes or mushrooms, fried or grilled onions, to go with eggs, bacon, sausages or French toast. For a real summer treat, include cooked asparagus or sweetcorn.

Liven up your mornings with these ideas or one of the special breakfast recipes on the following pages.

fruity muesli mix

A serving of muesli, which includes a tablespoonful of dried fruit, is simple and satisfying. Add fresh fruit and/or fruit juice to boost your total further. It's easy to make your own muesli mix using your favourite ingredients. Toasting the grains adds a delicious, nutty flavour.

500 g/1 lb porridge oats
250 g/8 oz flaked rice or other grains (from health shops)
50 g/2 oz sunflower seeds
50 g/2 oz pumpkin seeds
50 g/2 oz sesame seeds
50 g/2 oz hazelnuts, chopped
50 g/2 oz almonds, coarsely chopped
350 g/12 oz dried fruit (raisins, sultanas, chopped dates, chopped dried apricots)

Preheat the oven to 180°C/350°F/gas mark 4.

Put all the ingredients except the dried fruit into one or two large roasting tins. Bake for 20–30 minutes, stirring occasionally, until the nuts and grains are brown and toasted.

Allow to cool, then stir in the dried fruits.

Servings 12   Fruit/veg portions 12

munchy apple muesli

Get 2–3 of your daily portions of fruit in one bowl with this crunchy fresh muesli.

1 rounded tablespoon porridge oats
1 sweet apple, grated
juice of 1 orange
1 tablespoon raisins or sultanas
2–3 tablespoons thick yogurt
clear honey
1 tablespoon chopped hazelnuts, cashews or almonds

Mix the oats and apple with the orange juice and raisins or sultanas for a moist, juicy consistency.

Servings 1 Fruit/veg portions 2–3

Top with a dollop of yogurt, a drizzle of honey and hazelnuts, cashews or almonds

apricompote

Unsulphured dried apricots or, even better, the little bullet-hard Hunza apricots, both of which you can get from health food stores, are best for this recipe.

500 g/1 lb dried apricots
1 vanilla pod (optional)
850 ml/1½ pints of cold water

Put the apricots in a saucepan with the vanilla pod, if using.

Add the water, bring to the boil, reduce the heat and simmer gently for about 30 minutes until the apricots are very tender.

Remove the vanilla pod, rinse and dry (it can be used again).

Serve the apricot compote hot or cold with thick yogurt and a sprinkling of wheatgerm, chopped walnuts or pistachios.

Servings 4   Fruit/veg portions 4

Variation: Mixed Dried Fruit Compote can be prepared in the same way as the Apricompote, using a variety of dried fruits, such as 100 g/3½ oz each of apricots, prunes, figs, sultanas, dried peaches or pears. For a refreshing contrast, add fresh fruit, such as crisp apple, to the compote. You can also try sliced or chopped apple, pear, bananas, grapes, kiwi fruit or strawberries.

syrupy salad

Thick apricot or mango juice, sometimes called nectar, makes a glorious natural syrup for a fruit salad, which can be as varied as you like. This recipe gives one good portion of 'four plus' per person.

1 apple, peeled and chopped
2 kiwi fruit, peeled and sliced
1 banana, peeled and sliced
250 g/8 oz seedless grapes or hulled strawberries, halved if large
apricot or mango juice

Mix together the fresh fruit and moisten with the fruit juice.
Serve with yogurt and a scattering of toasted flaked almonds.

Servings 4 Fruit/veg portions 4

Thick apricot or mango juice makes a glorious natural syrup for a fruit salad

veggie french toast

Served with succulent grilled vegetables, French toast makes a nourishing breakfast or brunch dish.

2 or 3 flat mushrooms
1 egg
1 tablespoon milk
1–2 slices of bread, halved
1 tablespoon olive oil, plus more for brushing
1 tomato, halved
salt and freshly ground black pepper

Preheat the grill. Wipe the mushrooms, or wash and pat dry.

Beat together the egg and milk in a shallow bowl. Put the bread into the egg mixture, turn it and leave to soak up the liquid.

Brush the mushrooms with oil. Put them rounded-side up under the grill, turning them after 3–5 minutes to grill the other side. When you turn them, put the tomato halves under the grill and sprinkle with a little salt and pepper.

Heat the oil in a frying pan until hot but not smoking. Put in the bread and fry until golden brown on one side, then turn over and fry the other side. Serve at once with the mushrooms and tomato.

Servings 1 Fruit/veg portions 2

fruity french toasties

Served with a fruit topping, French toast is so luxurious – almost like starting the day with dessert. Soak the bread in the egg and milk mixture and cook in olive oil or butter, as described above.

Dust the French toast with ground cinnamon and a sprinkling of sugar (or with vanilla sugar) and top with a generous spoonful of apricot compote (see page 26).

Alternatively, cut a peeled banana in half crosswise and lengthwise and fry alongside the French toast. Serve with cinnamon and sugar sprinkled over or with a drizzle of clear honey.

Served with a fruit topping, French toast is so luxurious – almost like starting the day with dessert

sweetcorn fritters

These puffy little fritters make a nice change for a hot breakfast.
You can serve them with grilled tomatoes and mushrooms or, for a
'New World' flavour, with fried bananas, as in the preceding French
toast recipes. For this recipe, either raw or cooked sweetcorn cut
from 2 large or 3 small ears will do, or use a 225 g/8 oz can of
sweetcorn, drained.

200 g/7 oz fresh or thawed frozen sweetcorn kernels
50 g/2 oz plain flour
3 tablespoons milk
1 egg, separated
salt and freshly ground black pepper
pinch of cayenne pepper
1–2 tablespoons oil

Put the sweetcorn in a bowl and mix in the flour, milk and egg yolk.
Add a pinch of salt, a grinding of pepper and the cayenne.
Whisk the egg white until stiff and fold gently into the mixture.

Heat 1 tablespoon of the oil in a frying pan. Drop rounded
tablespoonfuls of the corn mixture into the pan, fry for a minute or
two until browned on one side, then flip over and fry the other side.

Continue until all the mixture has been used, adding a little more oil
to the pan, if needed. Serve at once.

Servings 2 Fruit/veg portions 2

breakfast stir-fry

A fresh take on breakfast onions, mushrooms and tomatoes, this stir-fry is made in less than five minutes. It tastes great with bacon, sausages and fried eggs, but is really at its best with creamy scrambled eggs and some hot buttered toast.

bunch of spring onions, roots trimmed
125 g/4 oz button mushrooms, wiped
225 g/8 oz cherry tomatoes, stalks removed
1 tablespoon olive oil
salt and freshly ground black pepper

Cut the spring onions into 1 cm/½ inch pieces (slicing them diagonally looks attractive) and use all the green part as well as the white.

Slice the mushrooms thinly and halve the cherry tomatoes.

Heat the olive oil in a large frying pan. Put in the spring onion, mushrooms and tomatoes and stir-fry over a high heat for 1–2 minutes until the mushrooms have cooked and the vegetables are heated through.

Season with salt and pepper and serve at once.

Servings 2–4 Fruit/veg portions 4

menu suggestions

Menu 1:

apricompote with thick greek yogurt (see page 26)

veggie french toast (see page 28)

darling clementine (see page 107)

Menu 2:

fruity muesli mix (see page 24)

breakfast stir-fry (see page 31)

strawberry orange delight (see page 108)

Menu 3:

thick yogurt with sliced peaches and raspberry jam

sweetcorn fritters (see page 30)

tropical smoothie (see page 107)

Breakfast is a good time to eat at least one portion of fruit or vegetables. Fresh fruit juice is a natural choice at this time of day. So is fresh fruit. But why not have both?

lunch

quick ideas

Get into the habit of eating a healthy lunch instead of grabbing a packet of crisps and you will feel the benefits very quickly. Salads featuring fruit and vegetables are an easy and enjoyable way to consume some of your five daily portions. These salads all pack well in a storage container with a tight-fitting lid.

Greek goodness
Mix chopped tomato, cubes of cucumber and feta cheese, mild red onion rings and black olives, and toss with vinaigrette dressing or olive oil and lemon juice. Serve with pitta bread.

Chef's traditional
Combine salad leaves and grated or chopped raw vegetables (carrots, celery, cucumber, peppers, and so on) with cherry tomatoes and slices of cheese, hard-boiled egg and cooked chicken or ham. Dress with vinaigrette or a creamy dressing, such as mayonnaise and yogurt stirred up with Dijon mustard.

Perfect with pasta
Moisten cooked pasta shapes (twists and bows are good) with vinaigrette or a yogurt-mayonnaise mixture and add a variety of colourful ingredients, including plenty of fruit and vegetables.

Some of my favourite combinations are: chopped red pepper, grated carrot, raisins and walnuts; chopped canned mandarin oranges in juice and chopped walnuts (popular with children), adding cooked chicken and chutney (for adults); chopped tomatoes, cucumber, celery, spring onions, sweetcorn kernels and tuna or prawns.

Easy cheesy
Stir chopped drained sun-dried tomatoes, halved cherry tomatoes,

shredded spring onions, black olives and diced Gruyère cheese into cooked pasta shapes, or substitute flaked Parmesan cheese and sprinkle on top with basil leaves.

Nice Niçoise
Combine cooked pasta shapes with crunchy-cooked French beans, tomato wedges, black olives and tuna; sprinkling with pine nuts and chopped herbs adds extra zest.

Cool couscous
Prepare couscous according to packet directions, season well, dress with lemon juice and olive oil and cool. Serve with grilled peppers and Italian leaves, chopped and stirred in with black olives. Mediterranean Couscous (see page 82) can be served cold, mixed and sprinkled with chopped mint.

Rice bowls
Use different kinds of cooked rice (a mixture of white and brown, perhaps with some wild rice or Camargue red rice as well), tossed in vinaigrette and mixed with fruit, vegetables and herbs.

Try some of the following combinations: grated carrots and toasted flaked almonds, flavoured with lemon rind and plenty of chopped chives, tarragon and parsley; chopped celery, spring onions, mango cubes and cooked chicken or duck; chopped celery, red pepper and spring onions, halved grapes and prawns.

Currying favour
Flavour cooked rice (Basmati is good) with curry powder and add diced celery, apple, banana, raisins, snipped dried apricots and roasted cashews or peanuts.

Mediterranean mix
Combine cooked rice with cold ratatouille, or mix in chopped tomatoes, crushed garlic, black olives and lightly cooked courgettes and aubergine. Top with snipped or torn basil leaves.

Bean feast
Add chopped red and green peppers, red onions, drained canned kidney or borlotti beans to cooked rice, flavour with ground cumin and coriander and sprinkle with chopped coriander leaves and, if you wish, pomegranate seeds.

Tasty tabbouleh
Prepare bulgur (cracked wheat) according to packet directions, season well and dress with lemon juice and olive oil. Stir in chopped red onion and tomato, cubes of cucumber and feta cheese, and lots of chopped mint and parsley, or use bought tabbouleh salad. Add black olives and avocado slices and serve with pitta bread.

pack a punch

Packed lunches provide plenty of ways to include fruit and veg: in sandwiches; fruit or veg-based main courses, perhaps with rice, pasta or couscous; in a small accompanying salad of crudités or tomatoes; or in a warming winter soup.

Here are some savoury sandwich ideas that are simple to make and must compete with that expensive deli around the corner.

Banana bonanza: Combine sliced banana with honey and a handful of chopped walnuts.

Nutty carrot: mix grated carrot with peanut butter or hummus.

Coriander hummus: chop fresh coriander and olives and add hummus.

Avocado dash: add a dash of tabasco to mashed avocado and spread liberally on bread.

Fruity cheese: mix canned-in-juice crushed pineapple or chopped dates with ricotta, quark or cream cheese.

Cheese roast: use up some leftover roasted veg in a tasty combo with ricotta, quark or smooth goat's cheese.

Mixed blessings: crisp lettuce or salad cress provides a great contrast for cream cheese, thinly sliced hard cheese, hummus, hard-boiled egg or flaked fish with mayonnaise–plain yogurt mix.

Cool contrast: stronger-tasting watercress or rocket is delicious with the creamy texture of sliced avocado.

Pitta coleslaw: fill a pitta bread or wholemeal bap spread with mayonnaise–yogurt mix or hummus, with shredded lettuce, cucumber, sliced tomato or home-made coleslaw (see page 137).

Racy red onion: butter bread with smooth rindless goat's cheese and fill generously with Tangy Red Onion Marmalade (see page 134); or try the tangy red onion marmalade with slices of traditional or smoked Cheddar cheese.

rose's rocket

Colourful peppers are easy to prepare and so versatile. The pungent rocket or basil leaves are perfect with the sweetness of the peppers, but peppery watercress is a good substitute.

1 large red pepper
1 large yellow or orange pepper
olive oil
balsamic vinegar
salt and freshly ground black pepper
85 g/3 oz rocket or basil leaves

Halve the peppers, remove the seeds and place rounded-side up under a hot grill for about 10 minutes until the skin is blistered and brown.

Cool, then peel off the outer papery skin (or leave it on, if you prefer). Slice the peppers into ribbons, mix with a little olive oil and a few drops of balsamic vinegar and season with salt and pepper.

Serve on rocket or basil leaves, drizzling the juices over.

Servings 2 Fruit/veg portions 5

crunchy beet salad

This salad offers a pleasant combination of flavours and textures: sweet, soft beetroot, peppery watercress, tangy goat's cheese and crunchy walnuts.

2 cooked beetroots, peeled (not pickled)
40 g/1½ oz prepared watercress (about ½ a packet)
100 g/3½ oz soft goat's cheese
2 tablespoons vinaigrette
freshly ground black pepper
8–12 walnut halves, roughly chopped

Slice the beetroots and arrange on two plates with the watercress.

Using two teaspoons, shape the cheese into small balls and nestle in the beetroot and watercress, dividing evenly.

Drizzle with vinaigrette, grind over some black pepper, scatter the walnuts and serve.

Stilton, or another blue cheese, can be substituted, crumbled or cut in cubes. The walnuts can be toasted for a few seconds under the grill, but this isn't essential.

Servings 2 Fruit/veg portions 2

classic waldorf

The classic Waldorf salad is usually popular with children, so can be a good way of getting them to eat some of their fruit and vegetables. Extra fresh or dried fruit or vegetables add interest and boost nutrition. This salad is best eaten fairly soon, although it does survive well in a lunch box, packed in a small, covered container.

2 sweet crisp apples
1 celery heart
juice of 1/2 a lemon
2 tablespoons thick yogurt
2 tablespoons mayonnaise
salt and freshly ground black pepper
25 g/1 oz walnuts or pecans, chopped
halved grapes, grated carrot, diced cucumber, raisins, sultanas, snipped
dried apricots or dates (optional)

Core and chop the apples and slice the celery.

Put them in a bowl with the lemon juice, yogurt and mayonnaise. Mix together and add seasoning to taste.

Stir in the nuts (or, if not serving immediately, add at the last minute to retain their crunchiness). Mix in any optional ingredients you wish and serve.

Servings 2 Fruit/veg portions 3 (optional additions extra)

cucumber and peanut salad

The flavours of fresh mint and coriander and spices make a wonderful combination in this fresh salad.

1 large cucumber
2 tablespoons roasted peanuts
1 tablespoon fresh coriander, chopped finely
1 tablespoon fresh mint, chopped finely
1 teaspoon caster sugar
1 tablespoon olive oil
1 teaspoon mustard seeds
1 teaspoon cumin seeds
1/2 teaspoon turmeric
2 dried chillies, broken up
1/2 teaspoon sea salt

Halve the cucumber and remove any large seeds, then grate the cucumber into a colander using the largest holes of the grater and squeeze out what moisture you can. Place in a bowl.

Grind the peanuts (salted or not according to taste) to a powder and add to the cucumber along with the coriander, mint and sugar.

Heat the oil in a small pan and put in the mustard and cumin seeds, turmeric, chillies and salt. When the seeds start to jump around, cover the pan and cook for a few seconds longer, then pour over the cucumber mixture. Serve at once. If you leave this salad, it will exude more liquid, which will spoil it.

Servings 2 Fruit/veg portions 4

supreme stilton salad

Crusty bread or hot toast goes well with this refreshing salad.

1 large ripe juicy pear
2 tablespoons vinaigrette
100 g/3 ¹/₂ oz Stilton cheese, rind removed
40 g/1 ¹/₂ oz prepared watercress (about ¹/₂ a packet)
freshly ground black pepper

Peel, core and slice the pear and toss in a little of the vinaigrette.

Slice the Stilton and arrange with the pear and watercress on two plates. Grind over some black pepper and serve.

Servings 2 Fruit/veg portions 2

For a hot variation, prepare as described, then put under a hot grill for a minute or two to melt the Stilton before serving

orange maple carrots

In this recipe the carrots need to be cooked until meltingly tender and glistening in their syrupy glaze. If preferred, you can use large carrots cut into batons.

15 g/½ oz butter
1 tablespoon maple syrup
1 teaspoon Dijon mustard
250 g/8 oz baby carrots, trimmed
4 tablespoons orange juice
salt and freshly ground black pepper
chopped flat-leaf parsley (optional)

Melt the butter in a large saucepan with the maple syrup, then stir in the mustard.

Add the carrots, orange juice and some salt and pepper. Stir to coat the carrots with the buttery mixture, cover and cook for 12–15 minutes until the carrots are very tender.

Check the seasoning and serve with a scattering of parsley.

Servings 2 Fruit/veg portions 3

roasted parsnips with lime

Roasted parsnips are sweet, crisp and easy to do. Small parsnips are best, though larger ones will do but need to be sliced into more pieces.

250 g/9 oz small parsnips
grated rind and juice of 1 lime
2 tablespoons olive oil
sea salt
freshly ground black pepper
lemon wedges

Preheat the oven to 200°C/400°F/gas mark 6. Scrub the parsnips if they are organic, peel them if not, then cut lengthways into halves or quarters depending on size.

Mix the lime juice and rind with the olive oil and brush this over the parsnips. Arrange them in a single layer on a roasting tray and pour any remaining lime mixture over them.

Bake for 40–45 minutes, or until they are browned and crisp outside and the point of a knife goes in easily. Sprinkle with sea salt and freshly ground black pepper.

Servings 2 Fruit/veg portions 3

Variations
roasted root veg
Try a mixture of root veg: chunks of swede, celeriac, parsnips and turnip, tiny potatoes and quarters of red onion. Use lemon juice and rind instead of lime and tuck some stems of thyme, rosemary or sage and a few unpeeled garlic cloves among the veg.

roasted sweet potatoes
Very yummy. Instead of parsnips, use scrubbed or peeled sweet potatoes, cutting them into quarters, sixths or eighths depending on their size.

Mediterranean roasted veg
Deseed and quarter 2 red peppers, cut 1–2 courgettes and 1 aubergine into chunky batons. Use lemon instead of lime, brush the veg as described (but there is no need to do the peppers as they'll cook well without oil). Add some herbs and whole unpeeled garlic cloves or some canned artichoke hearts, drained and halved. Black olives can be popped in about 10 minutes before the veg are done.

Roasting is such a simple and delicious way to prepare veg and takes minimal effort

japanese cauliflower

In this Japanese-style cauliflower recipe, the soft pink folds of pickled ginger contrast with the cauliflower both in colour and flavour. You can buy it at oriental food shops and some large supermarkets.

250 g/8 oz small cauliflower florets
1 tablespoon sesame oil
1 garlic clove, crushed
1 tablespoon light soy sauce
1 tablespoon pickled ginger, chopped
salt and freshly ground black pepper

Bring about 1 cm/$^1/_2$ inch of water to the boil in a large saucepan.

Add the cauliflower florets, bring back to the boil, cover and cook until the cauliflower is as you like it. It takes 4–5 minutes or a bit longer for the cauliflower to be tender but still retain some crunch, depending on the size of the florets.

Drain and return the cauliflower to the pan with the sesame oil, garlic, soy sauce and pickled ginger.

Season and serve.

Servings 2 Fruit/veg portions 3

spinach and cheese pasties

These taste amazing with a tomato salad and a sauce made by adding chopped chives or spring onions and some seasoning to thick yogurt.

500 g/1 lb tender spinach leaves, washed
100 g/3½ oz feta cheese, crumbled
salt and freshly ground black pepper
360 g/12 oz packet frozen puff pastry, thawed

Preheat the oven to 200°C/400°F/gas mark 6.

Cook the spinach, either in the packet in the microwave or in a dry saucepan, for 5–7 minutes until tender. Drain in a colander, pressing with the back of a spoon to remove as much liquid as possible. Mix with the crumbled feta cheese and season with salt and pepper.

On a lightly floured board, roll out the pastry as thinly as possible to make a piece 40 cm/16 inches square. (If you are using ready-rolled pastry, roll out to about double its size.)

Cut the pastry into 16 squares, 10 cm/4 inches on each side. Spoon some spinach mixture onto the middle of each piece of pastry, dividing it evenly. Brush the sides with water and press the edges firmly together, making triangular shapes.

Place the pastries on a baking sheet and bake for about 15 minutes, or until golden brown and crisp. Serve at once.

Makes 16 Fruit/veg portions 5

red onion and goat's cheese flan

This big flan makes a wonderful main course. Although it's large, there's never any problem eating it up – it's as good cold as it is hot. Serve with a leafy salad and mashed potato if you want a more substantial meal.

450 g/1 lb shortcrust pastry, bought or home-made (see page 140)
1 quantity Tangy Red Onion Marmalade (see page 134)
350 g/12 oz Somerset goat's cheese or French chèvre log

Make the Tangy Red Onion Marmalade as described on page 134 – this can be done well in advance as it will keep, covered, in the fridge for several days.

Preheat the oven to 200°C/400°F/gas mark 6. On a lightly floured board roll out the pastry and use to line a shallow (1 cm/1/2 inch deep) 30 cm/12 inch flan tin. Trim the edges, prick the base lightly and bake for 20 minutes until golden.

Spread the onion mixture evenly over the base of the flan. Cut the goat's cheese into thin slices and place on top of the onions, to cover them.

Cover the outer rim of the pastry loosely with strips of foil to prevent it burning, then put the flan under a preheated grill for 5–10 minutes to melt and brown the cheese.

Remove the foil strips and serve at once.

Servings 6 Fruit/veg portions 12

red peppers stuffed with feta

Classy as a starter to a posh meal or try it as a veggie main course served with lime-roasted parsnips or sweet potatoes. You can get the peppers at large supermarkets: they're often sold in pairs.

4 long pointed red peppers
200 g/7 oz feta cheese, drained
350 g/12 oz cherry tomatoes, halved
2 tablespoons pesto sauce
salt and freshly ground black pepper

Preheat the oven to 180°C/350°F/gas mark 4.

Cut the peppers in half: if you can cut through the stems so that you have half a stalk on each pepper half, so much the better. Scoop out the seeds and core and lay the pepper halves side by side in a roasting tin or large shallow casserole.

Cube the feta cheese and mix with the cherry tomatoes, pesto and some salt and pepper.

Divide this mixture between the pepper halves, then bake them for about 25 minutes, or until the peppers are tender, the tomatoes cooked and the cheese lightly browned.

Servings 4 Fruit/veg portions 8

leek and stilton pie

This lovely pie has a moist leek and Stilton filling and each serving contains two good portions of vegetables. The cheesy pastry is delicious and very quick to make, especially if you have a food processor. Or you could use frozen puff pastry instead (I suggest the ready-rolled type), using one of the pieces in the packet for the bottom of the pie and the other for the top.

750 g/1½ lb trimmed leeks, sliced
125 g/8 oz Stilton cheese, crumbled
salt and freshly ground black pepper

For the pastry:
250 g/8 oz plain wholemeal flour
125 g/4 oz butter, roughly chopped
50 g/2 oz freshly grated Parmesan cheese
1 egg yolk
pinch of salt
2 tablespoons water

Put the leeks into a saucepan with cold water to cover and bring to the boil. Boil for 8–10 minutes or until the leeks are tender.

Drain thoroughly in a colander (the water makes great stock, but you don't need it for this recipe). Mix the leeks with the Stilton cheese and salt and pepper to taste and set aside to cool.

Preheat the oven to 200°C/400°F/gas mark 6 and put in a baking sheet to heat up. To make the pastry, put the flour, butter, Parmesan, egg yolk and water into a food processor with a good pinch of salt and whiz just until a dough begins to form. Or put the dry ingredients into a bowl, rub in the flour with your fingertips until the mixture resembles breadcrumbs, then add the cheese, egg yolk and water and mix to make a dough.

Remove just under half the dough, knead it into a ball and roll out to fit a 32 cm/9 inch pie plate or shallow sandwich tin. Put the leek mixture on top of the pastry, trim the pastry edges to fit, then roll out the rest of the pastry and place on top.

Press down the edges, trim and crimp decoratively with your fingers or by pressing with the prongs of a fork. Make a steam hole in the centre of the top. Bake for 20–25 minutes until golden brown. If possible let the pie stand, out of the oven, for 5–10 minutes before cutting, to let the juices settle.

Servings 4 Fruit/veg portions 8

Each serving with its moist leek and Stilton filling contains two good portions of vegetables

quick ideas

Mouth-watering puddings are a really delicious way to eat a good portion of fruit, and even some cakes qualify, Although some fruit puddings take a little time and trouble to make, the pleasure with which they're received makes it worth the effort. There are plenty of quick puddings that you can make. Here are some ideas – more are included in the Supper Section.

Fresh fruit: Simply try a bowl of cherries or raspberries or serve luscious sweet ripe pineapple wedges cut across into sections for easy eating.

Brandied cherries: For quick brandied cherries, simply heat canned black cherries with a small glass of brandy.

Banana split: Peel a banana and cut in half lengthwise. Put vanilla ice cream between the two halves; top with grated or flaked chocolate or toasted hazelnuts.

Baked bananas: Bake unpeeled bananas in a moderate oven for about 10 minutes until tender and serve with vanilla ice cream.

Boozy pineapple: Peel a pineapple, cut out the central core and sprinkle slices with sugar and rum, brandy or kirsch. Grill until tender and lightly browned.

Apple alternatives: Mix cooked apple with thick Greek yogurt and crumble over shortbread. Or mix cooked apples with sultanas and grated orange rind.

tropical fruit salad

The secret of this scrumptious salad is to make sure that all the fruit is ripe. If necessary, shop a day or two in advance so it is really tender, sweet and fragrant.

1 ripe mango
1 ripe papaya
2 kiwi fruit
1 small ripe pineapple
a little honey to taste, optional

Make two cuts in the mango each about 5 cm/2 inches from the stalk, so that you cut down each side of the large flat stone. Then remove the peel and dice the flesh.

Peel the papaya, discard the seeds and dice the flesh.

Peel and slice the kiwi fruit and pineapple.

Mix all the fruits together in a bowl and sweeten with a little honey to taste.

Servings 2–4 Fruit/veg portions 8

red fruit compote

A mixture of red berries makes a compote packed with flavour: choose two or more in season and add sugar to taste. Some fruits, especially redcurrants, benefit from being heated.

125 g/4 oz redcurrants or blackcurrants, stems removed
125 g/4 oz raspberries
250 g/8 oz strawberries, hulled and sliced
125 g/4 oz blackberries or blueberries
50 g/2 oz caster sugar

Put all the fruits into a saucepan with the sugar and heat gently until the juices run and the fruits are slightly softened. Serve hot or cold.

Servings 4   Fruit/veg portions 6

A mixture of red berries make a compote packed with flavour

apple cake

A moist, light, fruity cake, this makes a good lunch-box filler and is also delicious served warm, with custard, yogurt or cream. You can use either cooking or dessert apples.

225 g/8 oz self-raising wholemeal flour
1 teaspoon mixed spice
125 g/4 oz butter
125 g/4 oz brown sugar
350 g/12 oz apples, peeled, cored and thinly sliced
125 g/4 oz currants
1 egg
2 tablespoons milk, or more

Preheat the oven to 150°C/300°F/gas mark 2. Grease and line a 23 cm/9 inch square tin.

Put the flour and mixed spice into a bowl, add the butter and rub in with your fingertips until the mixture resembles breadcrumbs.

Add the sugar, apple, currants, egg and milk and mix to combine well. The mixture needs to be quite soft, so that it drops easily from the end of the spoon, so add a little more milk if needed.

Put the mixture into the tin, level the surface and bake for 1 hour, or until it is firm and a skewer comes out clean. Cool on a wire rack and cut into 9 or 12 pieces.

Servings 9–12 Fruit/veg portions 6

rhubarb fool

Fruit fools – mixtures of tender cooked or ripe, mashed fruit swirled with whipped cream and yogurt – make luscious desserts and are so easy to do.

500 g/1 lb rhubarb, leaves removed
125 g/4 oz caster sugar
150 ml/5 fl oz double cream
150 ml/5 fl oz plain yogurt
1 teaspoon real vanilla essence

Unless the rhubarb is very young and tender, strip off any tough skin (it will peel off in long ribbons).

Cut the rhubarb into 2.5 cm/1 inch lengths and put into a saucepan with the sugar. Heat gently, uncovered, until the juices run and the sugar has dissolved in them, then cover and continue to cook gently for about 10 minutes, or until the rhubarb is very tender. Drain in a sieve (you won't need the juice).

Whisk the double cream and yogurt until the mixture stands in soft peaks. Gently fold in the rhubarb and vanilla essence and spoon into four dessert glasses.

Servings 4 Fruit/veg portions 4

Variations

Gooseberry

For gooseberry fool, either cook 500 g/1 lb topped and tailed gooseberries with sugar to taste or use two 300 g/10 oz cans, drained. Mash the gooseberries, then fold into the cream and yogurt mixture as described opposite.

Apple

Use 500 g/1 lb peeled and sliced cooking apples. Cook as described for rhubarb, adding 2 tablespoons of water. Mash the apples and fold into the cream and yogurt mixture.

Strawberry

This is easy because you don't have to cook the strawberries. Choose 500 g/1 lb of ripe, sweet strawberries. Hull them and mash with a fork. Sweeten with caster sugar to taste before folding into the cream and yogurt.

Mango

Mash the flesh from 1–2 large ripe mangoes with a fork or purée in a food processor. Mix with the cream and yogurt. A sprinkling of powdered cardamom is wonderfully fragrant in this.

date slices

These make a sweet and delicious snack or tea-time treat, and are also excellent as a pudding, when served warm with a dollop of yogurt or crème fraîche.

350 g/12 oz cooking dates
250 ml/8 fl oz water
1 teaspoon vanilla extract
225 g/8 oz butter
175 g/6 oz soft brown sugar
350 g/12 oz plain wholemeal flour
175 g/6 oz porridge oats
¼ teaspoon bicarbonate of soda
2 tablespoons water

Preheat the oven the oven to 180°C/350°F/gas mark 4. Grease and line a 23 cm/9 inch square tin.

Cut the dates into pieces, put them in a saucepan with the water and bring to the boil. Simmer gently for about 5 minutes until the dates have softened, add the vanilla essence and set aside to cool.

Meanwhile, cream the butter and brown sugar in a bowl or in a food processor. Mix in the flour and porridge oats.

Dissolve the bicarbonate of soda in the water, add to the flour mixture and mix well (by pulsing, if using a food processor).

Press half of this oaty mixture into the base of the prepared tin. Beat the dates until fairly smooth, then spread over the oat mixture. Top with the remaining oat mixture and press down well with the back of a spoon.

Bake for about 45 minutes until golden brown. Cool in the tin, then cut into pieces.

Makes 12 Fruit/veg portions 12

You'll find the dates for this recipe in the baking section of the supermarket. They may be pressed into a small block or packed loose in a bag. Either type is fine, but avoid the ones with extra sugar, sometimes called 'sugar-rolled'

pavlova roulade

This must be the dreamiest of puddings – a wicked way to get your fruit portions...

5 egg whites
250 g/9 oz caster sugar
1 tablespoon cornflour
1 teaspoon vinegar
25 g/1 oz flaked almonds
284 ml double cream
600 g/1 lb raspberries

Preheat the oven to 140°C/275°F/gas mark 1. Line a 28 x 33 cm/ 11 x 13 inch Swiss roll tin with a sheet of baking parchment.

Put the egg whites into a large, clean bowl and whisk until they are stiff and glossy – if you turned the bowl upside down they should be stiff enough not to fall out. Whisk in the sugar a tablespoonful at a time then fold in the cornflour and vinegar. Tip the mixture into the tin and gently level with a spatula.

Sprinkle flaked almonds on top and bake for 35 minutes. Cool in the tin. Just before you want to eat it, turn the roulade out, nut-side down, onto a piece of greaseproof paper. Strip off the baking parchment.

Whip the cream until stiff and spread over the roulade, then cover with the raspberries. With the long edges facing you, start to roll the one nearest you, using the greaseproof paper to help. Eat within 1–2 hours.

Servings 6   Fruit/veg portions 6

menu suggestions

Menu 1:

rose's rocket (see page 40)

red onion and goat's cheese flan (see page 50)
green salad leaves with versatile vinaigrette (see page 136)

pavlova roulade (page 62)

Menu 2:

minty green pea soup (see page 117)

red peppers stuffed with feta (see page 51)
roasted parnsips with lime (see page 46)

warm date slices with greek yogurt or crème fraîche
(see page 60)

Menu 3:

nutty pepper dip and crudités or breadsticks (see page 129)

spinach and cheese pasties (see page 49)
orange maple carrots (see page 45)

rhubarb fool (see page 58)

supper

quick ideas

Basing a main course on vegetables, or including them in it, for example in a hot pot, stew or chilli is one of the best ways of boosting your fruit and vegetable total for the day. There are many possibilities: here are some quick ideas followed by a wonderful selection of vegetable side dishes and supper recipes. More fruity sweet treat puddings follow.

Cheesy grill
Mix cooked vegetables, perhaps assorted root vegetables bought in a ready-prepared or frozen 'casserole' pack, boiled or microwaved, with a well-flavoured cheese sauce, sprinkle with cheese and/or breadcrumbs and brown under the grill.

Curried options
Microwave, steam or boil a selection of vegetables, mix with a jar of good quality curry sauce and serve with cooked rice, chutney, nan bread or poppadums and a side dish of sliced tomatoes, onions and lemon juice.

Chilli moments
Add a selection of quickly cooked vegetables to a jar of chilli sauce and a can of red kidney beans; serve with rice, soured cream and chopped avocado. Alternatively, try adding cooked cauliflower and cabbage to canned vegetable chilli or curry (all the major supermarkets sell their own brand). Serve with cooked rice and sliced tomatoes.

Salsa potatoes
Serve baked potatoes with salsa filling (chopped red onion, tomato, red pepper, lemon juice); pack them with coleslaw (see page 137) or shredded lettuce, cucumber and tomato; or with buttery or creamed cooked sweetcorn; or sautéed mushrooms; or lots of chopped parsley, spring onions and chives.

Pure pasta
Add roasted, grilled or steamed vegetables to freshly cooked pasta or rice.

Cheese bake
Prepare vegetables using red peppers, potatoes, sweet potatoes and purple onion slices. Ten minutes before they're done, top with slices of goat's cheese, feta cheese or very thinly sliced Halloumi. Bake until the cheese is lightly browned.

french peas

Cooking frozen peas in the French way gives them an extra dimension and makes them taste more like freshly podded peas. You can also cook fresh peas this way.

15 g/½ oz butter
1 tablespoon olive oil
6 spring onions, trimmed and chopped
1 lettuce
500 g/1 lb frozen petit pois or podded peas
2–3 carrots, sliced
2–3 small courgettes, sliced
large sprig of mint
pinch of sugar
salt and freshly ground black pepper

Melt the butter and olive oil in a large saucepan and add the spring onions.

Make a nest of lettuce leaves on top and put in the peas, carrots, courgettes and mint. Sprinkle with the sugar and some seasoning.

Cover the pan and cook over a gentle heat until all the vegetables are tender, about 15 minutes. Spoons are needed to enable you to eat every drop of the delicious juice.

Servings 4 Fruit/veg portions 8

spicy golden cauliflower and peas

Cauliflower need not be bland and dull. It absorbs flavours well, so add some spices, make sure you don't overcook it, and enjoy it at its best.

1 tablespoon olive oil
1 onion, peeled and chopped
1 garlic clove, crushed
1–2 teaspoons grated fresh ginger
1/2 teaspoon turmeric
1 teaspoon ground cumin
1 teaspoon ground coriander
250 g/8 oz cauliflower florets
6 tablespoons water
125 g/4 oz frozen petits pois
salt and freshly ground black pepper

Heat the oil in a large saucepan and put in the onion, garlic and ginger. Cover and cook gently for 7–8 minutes until the onion is soft.

Stir in the turmeric, cumin and coriander. Cook for a few seconds, then put in the cauliflower along with the water and some salt and pepper. Stir so that the cauliflower gets coated with the spicy mixture, then cover and cook for 4–5 minutes, or until the cauliflower is tender but still a little crunchy.

Add the peas and cook for a few seconds longer, just to heat them through, then check the seasoning and serve.

Servings 3 Fruit/veg portions 4

black bean broccoli

American nutritionists voted broccoli the most nutritious vegetable.
It's rich in calcium, as well as vitamins C and A, folic acid and iron.
Black bean sauce and toasted sesame oil give it a sweet oriental
flavour. Most supermarkets stock both.

1 tablespoon sesame oil
1–2 garlic cloves, crushed
2 teaspoons grated fresh ginger
250 g/8 oz broccoli florets
4 teaspoons black bean sauce
salt and freshly ground black pepper
1 teaspoon toasted sesame seeds

Heat the oil in a large saucepan and put in the garlic and ginger. Stir
for a few seconds, then put in the broccoli and stir-fry for a few minutes
until it is as tender as you like it.

Mix in the black bean sauce, season with salt and pepper and serve
sprinkled with the sesame seeds.

Servings 2 Fruit/veg portions 3

baby leeks with parsley

This dish can be served hot, warm or cold, and is particularly good as a first course or salad. Fatter, mature leeks can be used, but it's best with the little ones. Good quality, flavourful olive oil is essential. You can top this with some chopped or grated hard-boiled egg before serving.

250 g/8 oz trimmed baby leeks
1 tablespoon olive oil
juice of 1/2 lemon
salt and freshly ground black pepper
1–2 tablespoons chopped parsley, flat-leaf if possible

Put enough water in a large saucepan to cover the leeks and bring to the boil.

Add the leeks, cover and cook gently until they are very tender and easily pierced with a knife point or skewer. Drain (or keep the flavourful water for stock) and put the leeks back in the pan.

Add the olive oil and lemon juice, season with salt and pepper and mix gently. Sprinkle with parsley and serve.

Servings 2 Fruit/veg portions 3

Variations: Prepare the leeks as described above and add some juicy black olives and snipped red shards of sun-dried tomato for a Mediterranean flavour. Alternatively, garnish with breadcrumbs fried in olive oil and mixed with lemon rind and capers.

ginger swedes

A bit of chopped preserved ginger, the sort you buy in syrup in a glass jar, really livens up mashed swedes.

125 g/4 oz peeled swede, diced
125 g/4 oz prepared carrots, sliced
15 g/½ oz butter
1 piece preserved ginger, finely chopped
salt and freshly ground black pepper

Put the swedes and carrots in a saucepan with enough water just to cover and bring to the boil.

Cover the pan, boil gently until swedes and carrots are tender, then drain. Return the vegetables to the pan and mash with the butter, using a potato masher, or purée in a food processor.

Mix in the ginger and seasoning.

Servings 2 Fruit/veg portions 3

Variation: Include the same amount of parsnips, peeled and diced, along with the swede and carrots. Omit the ginger and mix in some freshly grated nutmeg and a tablespoonful of chopped parsley after mashing. This makes 3 servings.

roast butternut squash with raita

Roasting butternut squash, in it's skin, is an easy way to cook it and really brings out the flavour. The sharp yogurt raita complements the sweet orange flesh beautifully.

1 butternut squash
2 tablespoons olive oil
2 garlic cloves, crushed
1 teaspoon grated fresh ginger
1 teaspoon cumin seeds
salt and freshly ground black pepper
150 ml/5 fl oz plain yogurt
2 tablespoons chopped coriander

Preheat the oven to 200°C/400°F/gas mark 6.

Cut the butternut squash, unpeeled, into 5 cm/2 inch chunks, discarding the seeds. Combine the oil, garlic, ginger and cumin in a large bowl with some salt and pepper. Put in the pieces of squash and turn to coat.

Arrange the squash in a single layer, skin-side down, in a shallow baking dish and bake, uncovered, for about 40 minutes until they are very tender and easily pierced with a knife.

For the raita, mix the yogurt, coriander and salt and pepper to taste. Serve with the squash.

Servings 4 Fruit/veg portions 4

spinach and stilton crêpes

Serve with slices of tomato for extra colour and veg servings; add boiled baby new potatoes for a scrumptiously filling meal.

8–12 crêpes, bought or home-made (see page 141)
450 g/1 lb tender spinach leaves, washed
200 g/7 oz Stilton cheese
grated nutmeg

For the topping:
400g virtually fat-free fromage frais
50 g/2 oz Parmesan cheese, finely grated

Cook the spinach in its bag in the microwave or in a saucepan with no added water until it's tender – 4–7 minutes, depending on how tender it is in the first place.

Drain well and chop lightly, then mix with the Stilton, nutmeg and the seasoning.

Spoon some of the spinach mixture onto the crêpes, roll them up and place side by side in a shallow casserole.

Spread the fromage frais over the crêpes, scatter with the Parmesan and bake for 25–30 minutes until bubbling and golden brown. Alternatively, omit the fromage frais and just sprinkle with Parmesan.

Servings 4 Fruit/veg portions 4

wild mushroom galettes

The more interesting the mushrooms, the better these will be.

425 g/15 oz shortcrust pastry, bought or home-made (see page 140)
1 tablespoons olive oil
15 g/^{1}/$_2$ oz butter
450 g/1 lb wild mushrooms, sliced
2 garlic cloves, chopped
1 teaspoon cornflour
2 tablespoons lemon juice
4 tablespoons madeira or sherry
salt and freshly ground black pepper
4 tablespoons crème fraîche
1 tablespoon chopped chives

Preheat the oven to 200°C/400°F/gas mark 6. Divide the pastry into four equal pieces and roll each into a 12 cm/5 inch circle. Set aside.

Heat the oil and butter in a large saucepan, add the mushrooms and garlic and cook uncovered for 10–15 minutes until the mushrooms are tender and any liquid has disappeared.

Mix the cornflour with the lemon juice and madeira or sherry. Add to the mushrooms, stirring over the heat until the mixture has thickened slightly. Spoon the mixture onto the pastry circles. Press up the edges slightly, then bake for 20 minutes until the pastry is crisp.

Serve each galette topped with crème fraîche and chopped chives.

Servings 4 Fruit/veg portions 4

smoked cheddar mash pie

Cooked greens, such as lovely green winter kale or cabbage, go well with this and will up your vegetable count. The cider gives it a wonderful flavour, but you could use apple juice, milk or stock, if you wish, and omit the sugar.

25 g/1 oz butter
2 tablespoons flour
300 ml/10 fl oz cider (any type)
750 g/1½ lb prepared fresh or frozen casserole vegetables (carrot, swede, onion, leek)
1 tablespoon Dijon mustard
1 tablespoon demerara sugar
salt and freshly ground black pepper
1 kg/2 lb potatoes, peeled and cut into even-sized chunks
200 g/7 oz smoked Cheddar cheese, grated

Melt the butter in a large saucepan and stir in the flour. When it froths at the edges add the cider and cook, stirring frequently, until the sauce thickens and is smooth – 4–5 minutes.

Add the vegetables, cover and cook gently for 15–30 minutes until they are all tender.

Stir in the mustard and sugar, season to taste and keep the mixture warm until the potatoes are ready.

While the vegetables are cooking, boil the potatoes in water to cover until they are tender. Drain, keeping some of the liquid and mash with the cheese and the liquid to make a light consistency (they needn't be completely smooth – a rough texture is quite appealing). Season well.

Pour the vegetable mixture into a shallow casserole that will fit under your grill, spread the potato mixture over the top and put under a preheated grill for about 10 minutes, or until the potatoes are golden brown.

Servings 4 Fruit/veg portions 9

Using a packet of ready-prepared or frozen vegetables makes this recipe quick and easy

spicy vegetable chilli

This chilli is substantial on its own, but you could serve it over couscous or rice. Accompany with a leafy salad and crusty bread. If there's any chilli left over – it's even better the next day – try it rolled in tortillas, with some grated cheese and chopped avocado.

1 tablespoon olive oil
1 onion, peeled and chopped
1 garlic clove, crushed
1/2–1 teaspoon chilli powder
2 red peppers, deseeded and chopped
2 carrots, sliced
125 g/4 oz frozen sweetcorn
425 g/15 oz can chopped tomatoes in juice
425 g/15 oz can red kidney beans, drained
2 courgettes, diced
salt and freshly ground black pepper

Heat the olive oil in a large saucepan. Stir in the onion, cover and cook for about 7 minutes until softened.

Add the rest of the ingredients except the courgettes, stir well, cover and cook for 15 minutes.

Add the courgettes, cover and cook for a further 5 minutes or so until all the vegetables are tender. Season and serve.

Servings 4 Fruit/veg portions 16

vegetable tempura

Crisp, fresh vegetables deep-fried in batter make a perfect treat!

rapeseed, soya or ground nut oil for deep-frying
8 fresh baby sweetcorn, halved lengthwise
8 spring onions, trimmed and halved lengthwise
50 g/2 oz French beans, trimmed
1 large carrot, scraped and thinly sliced
1 red pepper, deseeded and cut into chunky sticks
50 g/2 oz cauliflower or broccoli cut into small florets
Japanese Dipping Sauce, for serving (see page 139)

For the batter:
125 g/4 oz plain flour
1 egg yolk
175–225 ml/6–7 fl oz cold water
salt and freshly ground black pepper

Heat the oil in a wok or saucepan (to 180°C/350°F if you have a cooking thermometer).

Put the flour and egg yolk into a bowl with some salt and pepper then add most of the water. Stir quickly – don't over-mix, the batter should be lumpy – and add the rest of the water if needed to make a batter thick enough to coat the veg thinly. Dip the veg into the batter and deep-fry a few at a time until golden brown and crisp. Drain on kitchen paper.

Serve at once – while crisp – with the Japanese Dipping Sauce.

Servings 4   Fruit/veg portions 8

creamy mangetout risotto

This is so warming and comforting. If you haven't got white wine or vermouth to hand, sherry or madiera – any cheap type – is also fine.

900 ml/1½ pints vegetable stock
1 tablespoon olive oil
bunch of spring onions, trimmed and chopped
2 garlic cloves, peeled and chopped
3 sticks of celery, finely chopped
275 g/10 oz risotto rice
2 glasses dry white wine or vermouth
250 g/9 oz trimmed mangetouts, sliced
50 g/2 oz butter
125 g/4 oz freshly grated Parmesan cheese
salt and freshly ground black pepper

Put the stock into a saucepan, bring to the boil and keep warm.

Heat the oil in a large, heavy-based saucepan over a medium heat; put in the spring onions, garlic and celery and fry gently for 7–10 minutes until they begin to soften.

Add the rice and stir over the heat for 1–2 minutes until the grains are coated with the juices. Still stirring, pour in the wine or vermouth and let it bubble away.

Add in a ladleful of the hot stock, continuing to stir over a moderate heat until it has been absorbed. Go on stirring and adding stock in this way for about 15–20 minutes until the rice is cooked – soft, but with a slight resistance. Add the mangetouts with the last of the stock.

Stir in the butter, Parmesan and salt and pepper. Cover and leave to stand for 2–3 minutes, then serve.

Servings 3–4 Fruit/veg portions 6

Variations: All kinds of vegetables can be added to risotto at the beginning of cooking, during cooking, or even when the cooking is done, depending on how long the vegetables take to cook. For instance, fry wild mushrooms, diced pumpkin or leeks with the onions and celery; or add tender spears of asparagus 8–10 minutes before the end of cooking.

All kinds of vegetables can be added to risotto at the beginning of cooking, during cooking or even when the cooking is done

mediterranean couscous

Grilling really brings out the flavour of vegetables and is quick and easy to do. You could also roast the vegetables in a hot oven.

1 medium aubergine
1 courgette
1 red pepper
1 red onion
2 tomatoes
juice of 1 lemon
olive oil
salt and freshly ground black pepper
250 g/8 oz couscous
chopped fresh basil leaves
black olives (preferably stoned)

Cut the aubergine in half lengthwise, then cut crosswise into slices about 6 mm/¼ inch thick. Slice the courgette into quarters or eighths lengthwise. Cut the pepper into quarters and discard the seeds. Peel the onion and cut into 6 mm/¼ inch thick rounds. Halve the tomatoes.

Mix the lemon juice with an equal quantity of olive oil and salt and pepper to taste. Brush the vegetables with this mixture and lay them on a grill pan. Grill until tender and lightly browned, turning them once.

Prepare the couscous according to the packet instructions. Season to taste, dress with a little olive oil and fork through the basil and olives. Serve with the grilled vegetables.

Servings 2 Fruit/veg portions 8

cheesy roast veg

This fresh and original way of serving veg is particularly good in winter but is equally useful at any time of year.

2 large sweet potatoes, scrubbed
2 large potatoes, scrubbed
2 carrots, scrubbed or scraped
1 large parsnip, peeled
2 red onions, peeled
2 tablespoons olive oil
juice of 1/2 lemon
2 garlic cloves, crushed
salt and freshly ground black pepper
250 g/9 oz Halloumi cheese
3–4 sprigs of rosemary

Preheat the oven to 200°C/400°F/gas mark 6.

Cut all the vegetables into chunky pieces and put in a single layer in a roasting tin or a very large ovenproof dish.

Mix the olive oil with the lemon juice and garlic, pour over the veg and toss them so they're all coated. Season with salt and pepper. Bake for 50 minutes until they're nearly done.

Drain the Halloumi and slice it as finely as you can. Put the Halloumi and rosemary all over the top of the veg and return to the oven for 15–20 minutes until the cheese is melted, lightly browned and crisp.

Servings 2–4 Fruit/veg portions 8

yummy dal

This is quick to make and wonderful with rice or warm bread or poured over boiled or steamed vegetables. Try it with some tomato and onion slices, and mango chutney.

1 tablespoon olive oil
2 onions, peeled and chopped
2–3 garlic cloves, chopped
250 g/8 oz split red lentils
pinch of cayenne
1 teaspoon ground cumin
2 teaspoons ground coriander
squeeze of lemon juice
salt and freshly ground black pepper
chopped fresh coriander, optional

Heat the oil in a large saucepan, put in the onion, cover and cook gently for 7–8 minutes until the onion is soft.

Stir in the garlic. Cook for a minute or two, then add the lentils and 750 ml/1^1/$_4$ pints water. Bring to the boil, stir, then leave to cook gently for 25–30 minutes until the lentils are pale and very tender.

Stir in the cayenne, cumin and coriander and season with salt, pepper and a squeeze of lemon juice to taste.

Serve hot or warm, sprinkled with chopped coriander if you're using this. This dal is even better reheated the next day.

Servings 2 Fruit/veg portions 8–10

thai coconut curry

This curry is wonderful when served with grilled chicken, marinated tofu or topped with a handful of crunchy roasted cashews.

125 g/4 oz carrots, cut into batons
2 large red peppers, deseeded and sliced
125 g/4 oz baby sweetcorn, halved diagonally
125 g/4 oz French beans, cut into 2 cm/1 inch lengths
125 g/4 oz broccoli florets
125 g/4 oz mangetout, halved diagonally
2 small pak-choi, sliced, or 125 g/4 oz baby spinach
4 tablespoons Thai red curry paste
400 g can coconut milk
salt and freshly ground black pepper
1 packet fresh coriander, chopped

Put the carrots and peppers into a large saucepan with 5 cm/2 inches of water, bring to the boil and simmer for 5–7 minutes until nearly tender. Add the sweetcorn, beans and broccoli and cook for a further 3 minutes; add the mangetouts and pak-choi or spinach and cook for 2 minutes.

Drain thoroughly and put the veg back in the pan with the Thai red curry paste, coconut milk and salt and pepper to taste. Stir gently and cook until the coconut milk is hot.

Add the coriander and serve. To boost protein, mix a tablespoonful of crunchy peanut butter with the coconut milk before adding or sprinkle some crushed roasted peanuts on top.

Servings 3–4 Fruit/veg portions 8

garlic cheese fusilli

Serve this creamy pasta with a leafy or tomato salad, and that's two of the day's portions of fruit and vegetables in a quick, easy and delicious form.

200 g/7 oz fusilli
salt
175 g/6 oz frozen petit pois
100 g/3½ oz garlic cream cheese (full fat or reduced fat)
freshly ground black pepper

Bring a large saucepan of water to the boil, add a tablespoonful of salt and the pasta. Cook until the pasta is tender but still a little resistant when you bite it (al dente). Reserve a ladleful of the cooking liquid.

Put the peas into a colander, drain the pasta over them and put all back into the still-warm saucepan.

Mix the cream cheese with a few spoonfuls of the reserved cooking water to make a creamy consistency, pour over the pasta and peas and toss gently.

Add some black pepper, check the seasoning and serve.

Servings 2   Fruit/veg portions 2

tempting tagliatelle

All kinds of cooked vegetables can be added to hot cooked pasta to make a delicious and healthy meal. This is one of my favourites.

200 g/7 oz tagliatelle
salt
250 g/8 oz asparagus
1 tablespoon olive oil
15 g/½ oz butter
175 g/6 oz oyster mushrooms, cut in bite-sized pieces
2 tablespoons chopped fresh parsley
fresh lemon juice
freshly ground black pepper
grated or shaved Parmesan cheese

Bring a large saucepan of water to the boil, add a tablespoonful of salt and the pasta. Cook until the pasta is al dente. Meanwhile, boil, steam or microwave the asparagus until it's just tender.

Heat the oil and butter in a saucepan and stir in the mushrooms. Cook for about 7 minutes or until tender; season with salt and pepper.

Drain the pasta and return it to the still-warm saucepan. Add the oyster mushrooms and their cooking juices, the asparagus, the chopped parsley and a squeeze of lemon juice.

Season with salt and pepper. Serve sprinkled with Parmesan.

Servings 2 Fruit/veg portions 4

peppery penne

The lively tomato sauce in this recipe contains about three portions of vegetables per person and you can increase it still further by serving it with a leafy salad.

200 g/7 oz penne
salt and freshly ground black pepper
1 tablespoon olive oil
1 onion, peeled and chopped
1 red pepper, deseeded and chopped
1 garlic clove, crushed
1 dried chilli, crumbled, or chilli powder to taste
425 g/15 oz can chopped tomatoes in juice
1 tablespoon drained capers
1 tablespoon chopped sun-dried tomatoes
2 tablespoons black olives, stoned
grated or flaked fresh Parmesan (optional)

Bring a large saucepan of water to the boil for the pasta.

Heat the oil in a medium saucepan and add the onion and red pepper. Stir, then cover and cook gently for 7 minutes until the vegetables soften.

Add the garlic, crumbled chilli or chilli powder, tomatoes, capers, sun-dried tomatoes and olives. Cook, uncovered, for 15–20 minutes, stirring occasionally, until the the sauce has thickened. Season with salt and pepper.

About 10 minutes before the sauce is ready, put the pasta into the boiling water, along with a tablespoonful of salt. Cook until the pasta is al dente. Drain the pasta and return it to the still-warm saucepan.

Either mix in the tomato sauce or toss the pasta in a tablespoonful of olive oil, serve it on warmed plates and pour the sauce on top. Serve the Parmesan separately if using.

Servings 2 Fruit/veg portions 8

Increase your vegetable quota by serving this lively tomato sauce dish with a leafy salad

supper puddings

It's great to round off a meal with a pudding, especially if it supplies some of your day's fruit and veg too. Here are some quick ideas.

Chocolate bananas

For a delectable treat, make a slit down the length of the banana cutting into the skin and flesh but not cutting the banana completely in half. Press squares of chocolate into the cut, wrap the banana in foil and bake or grill for 10–15 minutes until the banana is tender and the chocolate has melted to form a gooey sauce inside.

Mango sorbet

Make a quick mango sorbet by whizzing a 410 g can of mangos and their syrup to a purée and then freezing. This quantity serves two and is luscious eaten when it's frozen to a thick consistency but not icy solid. If it gets solid, leave it out of the freezer for half an hour or so then beat it before serving.

Fruit brûlée

For a quick brûlée, put ripe fruit, such as sliced peaches, raspberries or strawberries, into a shallow ovenproof dish and top with your choice of whipped double cream, half-and-half whipped cream and Greek yogurt or plain yogurt. Sprinkle with soft brown sugar and put under a hot grill until the sugar melts. Cool, then chill before serving. This is best when made with double cream as the yogurt versions tend to be a bit liquid round the edges and don't look as nice, although they still taste good.

Classic touch

Try revisiting the classic fruit and ice cream combinations, Peach Melba and Pears Belle Hélène. For Peach Melba, scoop vanilla ice cream on to really ripe skinned fresh peach halves or poached/canned peaches and top with home-made Raspberry Revival sauce (see page 130). For Pears Belle Hélène, top drained pears – canned or poached – with vanilla ice cream and Wicked Chocolate sauce (see page 131).

Frozen dates
Freeze fresh dates and eat without thawing: they taste like toffee.

moroccan orange and date salad

This combination of sweet juicy oranges and luscious dates is a winner. The orange flower water scents and flavours it intriguingly, but leave it out if you haven't any, or use a dash of orange blossom honey.

3 large oranges
150 g/5 oz fresh dates
orange flower water (optional)
a few fresh mint leaves

Cut the skin and pith away from the oranges in one long piece, using a sawing motion. Then cut the segments out from between the white membrane, working over a bowl to catch the juice.

Stone and halve the dates and add to the bowl along with a few drops of orange flower water and some fresh mint leaves.

Servings 3 Fruit/veg portions 4–5

cinnamon peaches

This is a delicious way to serve peaches that are a little under-ripe.

3 peaches
125 g/4 oz blackberries
125 g/4 oz blueberries
25 g/1 oz soft brown sugar
1/2 teaspoon ground cinnamon
juice of 1 orange
vanilla ice cream, for serving

Stone and slice the peaches. Put into a saucepan with the blackberries and blueberries.

Add the sugar, cinnamon and orange juice and heat gently until the peach slices are tender – 5–10 minutes.

Serve hot or cold with vanilla ice cream.

Servings 4 Fruit/veg portions 5–6

apple bake-over

One of the easiest hot fruit puddings, and one of the best – baked apples are good either hot or cold. Serve just as they are, warm from the oven, or with thick yogurt or cream. You could also stuff the apples with fresh or frozen blackberries and brown sugar instead of dates. Increase the recipe by the number of people you are serving.

1 large cooking apple
2–3 dried dates

Preheat the oven to 200°C/400°F/gas mark 6.

Remove the core from the apple and make a thin cut around the centre to prevent it bursting as it cooks. Stuff the dates into the core cavity.

Stand the apple in a shallow casserole or roasting tin and bake, uncovered, for about 45 minutes or until tender.

Servings 1 Fruit/veg portions 2

Stuff them with dates or fresh blackberries and slather with thick yogurt or cream

honey-baked pears

For an even fancier treat, serve these with ginger ice cream, thick yogurt or cream, or a raspberry sorbet.

4 pears
2 tablespoons honey
1–2 vanilla pods (optional)

Preheat the oven to 170°C/325°F/gas mark 3.

Peel the pears, keeping them whole with stems intact. Lay them in an ovenproof casserole dish, drizzle over the honey and tuck in the vanilla pods if you're using them.

Cover with foil or a lid and bake for 1 hour or until the pears are completely tender. Serve hot or cold.

Servings 4 Fruit/veg portions 4

Serve these with ginger ice cream, thick yogurt or cream, or a raspberry sorbet

summer pudding

This warm weather favourite is glorious when made with fresh ripe fruit.

500 g/1 lb raspberries
250 g/8 oz redcurrants, stems removed
250 g/8 oz blackcurrants, stems removed
125 g/4 oz caster sugar
8 large slices of white bread, crusts removed

Put all the fruits into a saucepan with the sugar and 3 tablespoons of water and heat gently until the juices run and the fruits are slightly softened – about 4 minutes. Remove from the heat and drain the juice.

Reserve one of the pieces of bread. Cut the rest in half to form rectangles. Trim the reserved slice to a circle the same size as the base of a 1.5 litre/2^1/$_2$ pint pudding basin. Dip the circle of bread in the juice and put it in the basin.

Arrange the bread rectangles around the basin, dipping them in the juice before placing and leaving some for the top. Put the fruit into the bread-lined bowl, adding a little of the juice to make a moist mixture. Save any leftover juice.

Cover with the remaining bread slices. Put a saucer on top of the basin and a weight to hold it down. Chill in the refrigerator for several hours. To serve, invert a plate over the top of the basin and, holding them tightly together, turn the basin upside down. Shake firmly several times until the pudding comes out. Pour any leftover juice over the top.

Servings 4 Fruit/veg portions 10

veiled country girl

This traditional Danish pudding is a delectable way to enjoy apples (with sweet apples less sugar is needed). The jam is traditional but you can leave it out and simply make two layers of apple.

900 g/2 lb apples
finely grated zest and juice of 1/2 lemon
about 75 g/3 oz caster sugar
40 g/1¹/₂ oz butter
175 g/6 oz dry bread, made into crumbs
175 g/6 oz raspberry jam, or other red jam
150 ml/5 fl oz double or whipping cream (or thick yogurt)

Peel, core and slice the apples. Put them into a saucepan with the lemon juice and rind, cover and cook gently for about 10 minutes until tender. Or put them into a shallow casserole dish, cover and microwave until tender; this may also take about 10 minutes. Stir in sugar to taste, depending on how sharp the apples are, and beat with a spoon to make a purée.

Melt the butter in a large frying pan, saucepan or wok. Add the breadcrumbs and 1 tablespoonful of caster sugar. Cook gently for about 6 minutes until the crumbs are crisp and brown, stirring occasionally.

Put a layer of crumbs into a deep glass dish, using about one-third, and spoon in the apple purée. Sprinkle over another third of the crumbs, then spread the red jam over the top and finish with a final layer of crumbs.

Servings 4   Fruit/veg portions 8

pear tarte tatin

You can prepare this in advance and have it ready for baking just before the meal.

200 g/7 oz ready-rolled puff pastry
6 medium pears
40 g/1¹/₂ oz butter
40 g/1¹/₂ oz caster sugar

Preheat the oven to 200°C/400°F/gas mark 6. Line the base of a shallow 20 cm/8 inch cake tin with a circle of baking parchment. Cut a circle of pastry 1 cm/¹/₂ inch larger than the tin and set aside.

Peel, quarter and core the pears. Melt the butter and sugar gently in a large saucepan and add the pear quarters. Cook over a moderate to high heat for 6 minutes, stirring often, until the pears are very lightly browned.

Arrange the pears rounded-side down in the baking tin and tuck the cinnamon in among them, making sure you transfer as much of the buttery mixture as possible. Leave to cool a little, then put the pastry on top, tucking it down into the pears at the sides.

Make several steam holes in the pastry and bake for 20 minutes. Leave it to stand for 3–4 minutes, then carefully invert it onto a large plate.

Servings 6 Fruit/veg portions 6

plum crumble

Any red fruits, such as redcurrants, raspberries or strawberries, as well as gooseberries or rhubarb, can be used to make a crumble. Most need to be cooked before you add the crumble topping, but plums (and rhubarb) need no pre-cooking, so this recipe is extra quick.

900 g/2 lb plums, halved and stones removed
ground cinnamon, for sprinkling
75 g/3 oz caster sugar

For the crumble topping:
200 g/7 oz self-raising flour (half wholemeal is nice)
150 g/5 oz demerara sugar
100 g/3½ oz butter, roughly chopped

Preheat the oven to 200°C/400°F/gas mark 6. Put the fruit into a shallow ovenproof dish and sprinkle over some cinnamon and the caster sugar.

To make the crumble topping, put the flour, demerara sugar and butter into a food processor and whiz until crumbly. Or put the flour and butter into a bowl, rub in the butter with your finger tips, then stir in the sugar.

Spoon the crumble mix over the top of the fruit and bake for 30–40 minutes or until the fruit is tender and the crumble lightly browned.

Servings 6   Fruit/veg portions 8

choc fondue with strawberries

A decadently easy way to eat 1–2 portions of fruit...

50 g/2 oz chocolate, plain or milk
2–4 tablespoons cream, single or double
125–225 g/4–7½ oz strawberries, washed but still with their green bits

Break the chocolate into a china or glass bowl or serving dish and melt in the microwave; or set the bowl over a pan of boiling water until the chocolate has melted.

Remove from the heat and gently stir in the cream to make the mixture as soft as you want.

Put the strawberries into another bowl and serve with the fondue.

Servings 1 Fruit/veg portions 1–2

Try this delicious fondue with skinned slivers of ripe pear, sweet ripe cherries, mandarin or satsuma segments

apricot medley

Serve as pudding or after-dinner treat, with peppermint tea or Turkish coffee for a Middle Eastern touch.

200 g/7 oz ready-to-eat dried apricots
2 teaspoons honey
1 teaspoon vanilla extract or essence
25 g/1 oz shelled pistachio nuts, finely chopped

Put the apricots into a food processor and whiz to a purée. Add the honey and vanilla and whiz again.

Spread the chopped pistachio nuts out on a plate, put teaspoons of the apricot mixture on top of the pistachio nuts, then form the apricot mixture into balls, coating them in the nuts.

Servings 12 Fruit/veg portions 6–7

Serve this recipe with peppermint tea or Turkish coffee for a Middle Eastern flavour

menu suggestions

Menu 1:

cheesy roast veg (see page 83)

creamy mangetout risotto (see page 80)
leafy salad or tomato salad

honey-baked pears with ginger ice cream (see page 94)

Menu 2:

baby leeks with parsley (see page 71)

tempting tagliatelle (see page 87)

moroccan orange and date salad (see page 91)

Menu 3:

wild mushroom galettes (see page 75)

spinach and stilton crêpes (see page 74)
french peas (see page 68)

veiled country girl (see page 96)

around the
the
clock

all day long

Juices, soups, snacks and dips are great for topping up fruit and veg quota mid-morning, mid-afternoon or at any time of day (or night!).

jump for juices

Juices and drinks are a fantastic way of getting in at least one portion of daily fruit and veg, even if you're not crazy about them. An extra glass or two is a quick and simple way to raise your fruit and veg intake.

Why not serve orange juice at breakfast, some apple juice with sparkling water in the afternoon or a glass of tomato juice perked up with Tabasco, Worcestershire sauce, a slice of lemon, or even a dash of vodka in the evening. Juice from a packet, can or bottle is fine, but make sure the label says 'pure juice' and not 'fruit juice drink', which may contain little actual juice.

If you enjoy juices, be adventurous and try making some luxurious smoothies, frothy milk shakes and blended drinks. These can be delicious and the only piece of equipment you need is a blender.

Real juice enthusiasts may want to invest in a juicer. Home-made juice tops the bill for flavour and vitamins, even though you need quite a lot of fruit and veg to make a modest amount of juice. While a juicer can be fiddly to wash, the trick is to do it immediately after making the juice, and before drinking it, while the discarded pulp is still moist enough to be rinsed away quickly and easily.

sunrise cocktail

A gorgeously coloured juice – just like a sunrise in a glass.

225 g/8 oz pineapple flesh
225 g/8 oz carrots, scrubbed if organic, peeled if not
125 g/4 oz raspberries

Cut the fruit and vegetables to fit your juicer. Juice and use immediately.

Servings 1 large glass Fruit/veg portions 2

three-fruit smoothie

Banana adds a creamy texture to the tangier flavours of pineapple and strawberries.

50 g/2 oz hulled strawberries
50 g/2 oz pineapple flesh
1 banana, peeled and sliced
4 ice cubes

Put all the ingredients into a blender or food processor. Cover and whiz until smooth. Pour into a glass and serve.

Servings 1 large glass Fruit/veg portions 2

strawberry ice smoothie

Make this with fresh strawberries if possible but frozen strawberries will do. The thick, creamy pink drink is like a fabulous ice cream soda.

85 g/3 oz hulled strawberries
250 ml/8 fl oz milk
1 tablespoon sugar, honey or maple syrup

Put the strawberries into a blender or food processor with the milk and the sugar, honey or syrup. Cover and whiz until thick and creamy. Taste and add a little more sweetening if needed. Serve at once.

Servings 1 large glass Fruit/veg portions 1

watermelon ginger

Use the puréed ginger you can buy in little jars – very labour-saving.

250 g/8 oz watermelon flesh, seeds removed
1 tablespoon grated fresh ginger
6 ice cubes

Put all the ingredients into a blender or food processor. Cover and whiz together to a thick vibrant red purée. Add cold water to thin a little.

Servings 1 large glass Fruit/veg portions 2–3

tropical smoothie

All the fruit should be ripe for this exotic drink.

1 banana
1 papaya
1 small ripe pineapple
1 small mango
8 ice cubes

Peel all the fruit and remove the seeds. Discard the central core of the pineapple. Cut the fruit into even-sized pieces and put into a blender or food processor with the ice. Cover and whiz to a thick, smooth purée, adding water to get the desired consistency. Serve at once.

Servings 4 Fruit/veg portions 8

darling clementine

225 g/8 oz apple
225 g/8 oz pear
2 clementines (or satsumas), peeled

Cut the fruit and vegetables to fit your juicer. Juice and use immediately.

Servings 1 large glass Fruit/veg portions 2

pineapple and mango punch

This tasty drink packs a healthy punch with 3 portions of fruit.

125 g/4 oz peeled fresh mango or drained and rinsed canned mango
300 ml/10 fl oz pineapple juice

Put all the ingredients into a blender or food processor. Cover and whiz to a thick golden purée. Pour into a glass and serve.

Servings 1 large glass Fruit/veg portions 3

strawberry orange delight

Fresh and vibrant, this juice is the perfect wake-up drink and a great morning tonic at the weekends.

125 g/4 oz hulled strawberries
150 ml/5 fl oz orange juice

Put all the ingredients into a blender or food processor. Cover and whiz until smooth. Pour into a glass and serve.

Servings 1 large glass Fruit/veg portions 2

creamy banana shake

Chocaholics can add 1 teaspoon of cocoa powder and 1 teaspoon of sugar to the ingredients below.

1 banana, peeled and sliced
125 ml/4 fl oz plain yogurt
1 teaspoon vanilla extract
4 ice cubes

Put all the ingredients into a blender or food processor. Cover and whiz until thick and creamy. Serve at once.

Servings 1 large glass Fruit/veg portions 1

strawberry banana smoothie

125 g/4 oz hulled strawberries
1 banana, peeled and sliced
8 ice cubes
grated rind and juice of 1 lime

Put all the ingredients into a blender or food processor. Cover and whiz to obtain a thick purée. Pour into a glass and serve.

Servings 1 large glass Fruit/veg portions 2

blackcurrant smoothie

Sneak in 1–2 portions of fruit with this creamy drink. You can use soy milk if you prefer.

210 g/7$^{1}/_{2}$ oz can blackcurrants in apple juice
200 ml/7 fl oz milk
1 tablespoon sugar, honey or maple syrup

Put the blackcurrants, along with their juice, into a blender or food processor with the milk and sugar, honey or maple syrup. Cover and whiz until thick and creamy. Sieve into a glass and serve.

Servings 1 large glass Fruit/veg portions 1–2

four-star top-up

250 g/8 oz carrots, scrubbed if organic, peeled if not
125 g/4 oz celery
125 g/4 oz apples
a few sprigs of parsley

Cut the fruit and vegetables to fit your juicer. Juice and use immediately.

Servings 1 large glass Fruit/veg portions 2

carrot with a ginger top

Ginger adds a zappy flavour to this brightly coloured vegetable drink.

500 g/1 lb carrots, scrubbed if organic, peeled if not
2 teaspoons grated fresh ginger

Cut the carrots to fit your juicer. Juice the carrots, add the ginger, and use immediately.

Servings 1 large glass Fruit/veg portions 2

five-star ruby

This glorious deep ruby juice is sweet and appeals to children.

250 g/8 oz carrots, scrubbed if organic, peeled if not
125 g/4 oz pineapple flesh
125 g/4 oz apples
1/2 cucumber
1 small beetroot, scrubbed if organic, peeled if not

Cut the fruit and vegetables to fit your juicer. Juice and use immediately.

Servings 1 large glass Fruit/veg portions 2–3

aperitifs

Juice-based drinks, with or without alcohol, make a refreshing
pre-dinner aperitif or are ideal to enjoy in the garden on long summer
evenings. All can help boost the daily fruit quota – 100 ml/4 fl oz of
juice equals a fruit portion. Here are a few suggestions for a relaxing
treat at the end of the working day.

virgin mary
Fill a glass with ice cubes, top up with tomato juice, shake in a generous
amount of Worcester sauce and tabasco, stir and serve. For a Bloody
Mary add a slug of vodka to the glass.

red lady
Mix 50 ml/2 fl oz each of cranberry juice and red orange juice; add a
generous slug of vodka and angostura bitters to taste. This is the
equivalent of a generous portion of fruit, depending on the type of
cranberry juice you use – most cranberry 'drinks' contain under 25 per
cent of the actual juice.

bucks fizz
Mix equal parts of freshly squeezed orange juice and Champagne or
sparkling white wine. The flavour and colour are fantastic when this is
made with red orange juice.

mulled apple juice
Put 1 litre of still apple juice into a large saucepan with an orange
stuck with 6 cloves, a bay leaf, half a cinnamon stick, $1/2$ a teaspoon
of ground ginger and $1/2$ a teaspoon ground nutmeg. Bring to the boil,
then leave over a gentle heat for 15 minutes. This equates to 10
fruit portions.

tropical lime smoothie

1 banana, peeled and sliced
150 ml/5 fl oz pineapple juice
grated rind and juice of ½ lime

Put all the ingredients into a blender or food processor. Cover and whiz to a thick golden purée. Pour into a glass and serve.

Servings 2 large glasses Fruit/veg portions 2

pineapple ginger

125 g/4 oz pineapple flesh
300 ml/10 fl oz ginger beer

Put all the ingredients into a blender or food processor. Cover and whiz until smooth. Pour into a glass and serve.

Servings 2 large glasses Fruit/veg portions 1

papaya colada

½ ripe papaya, peeled and deseeded
1 tablespoon coconut milk powder
300 ml/10 fl oz pineapple juice
pulp from 1 passion fruit

Put all the ingredients into a blender or food processor. Cover and whiz to a thick purée. Pour into a glass and serve.

Servings 1 large glass Fruit/veg portions 3

sunset smoothie

Get four of your fruit and veg portions in one go with this refreshing smoothie the colour of a summer sunset. Enjoy it sweet and natural, or pep it up with a dash of white or dark rum for an extra kick.

150 ml/5 fl oz pure squeezed red orange juice
250 g/8 oz sweet pineapple flesh
1 measure of rum (optional)
4 ice cubes

Put all the ingredients except the ice into a blender or food processor, cover and whiz until smooth. Pour into a glass, add the ice cubes and serve.

Servings 1 large glass Fruit/veg portions 4

Now you have blended some of the juices in this chapter, why not experiment to create your own fruit and veg combinations?

super soups

If you're seeking an easy-to-eat format for veg, why not try soups? Even people who will not or cannot eat veg in other forms often enjoy them in soups, and these are quick and easy to make. Begin by sweating chopped onion and potato gently in butter or oil – the onion for flavour, the potato for thickening. Add another main vegetable, along with water or stock, then simmer until the vegetables are tender enough to whiz to a purée in a blender or food processor, or with a hand-held blender put straight into the pan. The soup can be left chunky if preferred.

This simple method works well for most veg and, once you get the hang of it, you can rustle up soup very quickly. Stock isn't always necessary – I prefer the pure flavour of vegetables rather than that of added stock cubes or powder. But if you need a flavour boost, there are some good stock mixes on the market. Another thing I sometimes do is to make 'lazy stock' at the same time as the soup by adding a carrot, a piece of celery and some sprigs of herbs to the water, then removing them before puréeing the soup.

If you make soup often, a pressure cooker might come in useful. Modern ones are safe and very easy to use and they reduce cooking time by about a third so you can make beautiful soup from start to finish in 20–30 minutes. Leftover soup freezes well, but remember to get it out of the freezer in good time as it takes ages to thaw.

In winter, soups make a warming and satisfying lunchtime meal. If you have a hectic work schedule, these can be pre-prepared and taken to work in a vacuum flask. Or, in summer, iced soup works just as well.

minty green pea soup

This can be thrown together on the spur of the moment and is ready in minutes. Just make sure you have an onion on hand and some peas in the freezer.

15 g/½ oz butter
1 onion, finely chopped
500 g/1 lb frozen petit pois
1.2 litres/2 pints water or stock
several sprigs of fresh mint
salt and freshly ground black pepper
chopped mint

Melt the butter in a large saucepan, add the onions, cover and cook gently, without browning, for 5 minutes.

Add the peas, the water and the leaves from the mint sprigs. Bring to the boil, reduce the heat and simmer for about 5 minutes or until the peas are tender.

Put the soup into a blender, cover and whiz to a bright green purée. Season to taste. Serve with chopped mint sprinkled on top.

Servings 4 Fruit/veg portions 5

golden pumpkin soup

The warm flavour of ginger gives extra tang to this lovely golden soup.

1 tablespoon olive oil
1 onion, finely chopped
2 garlic cloves, crushed
3 cm/1¼ inch piece fresh ginger, peeled and finely chopped
650 g/1¼ lb peeled pumpkin or squash flesh
850 ml/1½ pints water or stock
salt and freshly ground black pepper
chopped chives

Heat the oil in a large saucepan, add the onions, cover and cook gently, without browning, for 5 minutes. Stir in the garlic, ginger and pumpkin, cover and leave to cook for a further 5 minutes.

Add the water or stock, bring to the boil, reduce the heat and simmer for about 15 minutes, or until the pumpkin is very tender.

Put the soup into a blender or food processor, cover and whiz to a purée. Add a little more water or stock if you want the soup thinner, then season to taste.

Serve topped with chopped chives.

Servings 4 Fruit/veg portions 6

iced beetroot soup

This is such a quick soup to make, and each serving supplies two portions of vegetables. You need beetroot, which has been prepared without vinegar: vacuum-packed cooked beetroot is fine. If you can't get dill, use chopped chives instead. Warm rye bread goes well with this recipe.

250 g/9 oz cooked skinned beetroot
700 ml/1½ pints tomato juice
salt and freshly ground black pepper
squeeze of lemon juice
150 ml/5 fl oz soured cream
2 tablespoons roughly chopped dill

Cut the beetroot into large chunks. Put the chunks into a blender or food processor with the tomato juice and whiz until smooth.

Season with salt, pepper and a squeeze of lemon juice.

Transfer the mixture to a bowl or jug and chill thoroughly. At the same time, put four soup bowls into the fridge and chill these too.

To serve, divide the soup among the bowls and top each with a spoonful of soured cream and some chopped dill.

Servings 4 Fruit/veg portions 8

mexican bean soup

The ingredients here make two big bowls of brick-red soup, filling
and satisfying enough for a main course and supplying two people
with two portions of daily fruit and veg. As a starter, in smaller bowls,
there's enough for four, each containing one daily portion. A selection
of garnishes served on the side makes a festive meal.

1 tablespoon olive oil
1 onion, peeled and chopped
1 carrot, diced
1 stalk of celery, diced
1 garlic clove, chopped
1 bay leaf
1/2 teaspoon ground cumin
1 teaspoon ground coriander seeds
1 teaspoon oregano
425 g/15 oz can red kidney beans, drained and rinsed
425 g/15 oz can chopped tomatoes in juice
850 ml/11/2 pints of water
salt and freshly ground black pepper
fresh lemon juice
garnishes: chopped spring onions, chopped fresh coriander, sour cream,
  crème fraîche, chopped red pepper, chopped avocado, lime wedges
  (all optional)

Heat the olive oil in a large pan and add the onion, carrot, celery
and garlic. Cover and cook over a gentle heat for 10 minutes, stirring
occasionally, until the vegetables are beginning to soften.

Add the bay leaf, cumin, coriander and oregano and stir well, then put in the beans, tomatoes and water. Bring to the boil, reduce the heat and simmer gently for 20–30 minutes or until the vegetables are very tender.

Remove the bay leaf. Purée about half of the soup in a food processor or blender, return to the pan and season with salt, pepper and a squeeze of lemon juice. Serve piping hot.

Servings 2–3 Fruit/veg portions 8

The ingredients make enough of this brick-red soup for two filling and satisfying main courses or starters for four people. Garnishes served on the side add a festive touch

sweetcorn chowder

Quick and simple to make, this is a real 'comfort' soup that slips down very easily. You can use kernels cut from fresh sweetcorn, frozen sweetcorn kernels or even canned sweetcorn, but choose the type that has been canned without added salt and sugar.

25 g/1 oz butter
1 large onion, peeled and chopped
500 g/1 lb potatoes, peeled and cut into 1 cm/^{1}/$_2$ inch dice
450 ml/16 fl oz full cream milk
450 ml/16 fl oz vegetable stock
350 g/12 oz sweetcorn kernels
salt and freshly ground black pepper
2 tablespoons chopped parsley

Heat the butter in a large saucepan and stir in the onion and potatoes. Cover and cook gently, without browning, for 10 minutes.

Add the milk and stock and bring to the boil. Reduce the heat, cover and boil gently for a further 5–10 minutes until the potatoes are almost tender.

Season with salt and pepper. If you wish to thicken the soup, liquidise a good ladleful or two, stir it back in and reheat. Sprinkle with parsley before serving.

Servings 4 Fruit/veg portions 4

spinach and chickpea soup

This is a quick version of a traditional Spanish peasant soup. It's very filling and warming and is usually redolent with garlic, but use less if you wish. Serve with crusty bread or chunky croutons made by cutting thick fried bread into 1 cm/^{1}/$_2$ inch squares.

1 tablespoon olive oil
1 onion, finely chopped
4–8 garlic cloves, chopped
1 potato, peeled and cut into 1 cm/^{1}/$_2$ inch dice
425 g/15 oz can chick peas
500 g/1 lb spinach, washed
1.2 litres/2 pints water or stock
salt and freshly ground black pepper

Heat the oil in a large saucepan. Add the onion, cover and cook gently, without browning, for 5 minutes.

Add the garlic and potato, stir, cover again and leave to cook for a further 5 minutes.

Pour in the chick peas, with their liquid, the spinach and water or stock. Bring to the boil, reduce the heat and simmer for about 15 minutes until the potato is tender.

Season to taste with salt and pepper.

Servings 4   Fruit/veg portions 8

spicy parsnip soup

Parsnips respond well to spices. Here I've just used ordinary curry powder to keep things simple, although you could use a teaspoonful of ground cumin and two teaspoons of ground coriander.

1 tablespoon olive oil
1 onion, finely chopped
1–1½ tablespoons curry powder
500 g/1 lb parsnips, peeled and cut into small dice
850 ml/1½ pints water or stock
1 tablespoon double cream
salt and freshly ground black pepper
squeeze of lemon juice
chopped chives

Heat the oil in a large saucepan, add the onions, cover and cook gently, without browning, for 5 minutes. Stir in the curry powder and parsnips, cover and leave to cook for a further 5 minutes. Then add the water or stock, bring to the boil, reduce the heat and simmer for about 15 minutes, or until the parsnips are very tender.

Put the soup into a blender or food processor with the cream, cover and whiz until smooth. Add a little more water or stock if you want the soup thinner.

Season to taste with salt, pepper and a squeeze of lemon juice and serve topped with chopped chives.

Servings 3–4 Fruit/veg portions 4

quick snack ideas

Little and often is a positive way to eat food and keeps your metabolism on red alert. Why not use the traditional mid-morning coffee-break or afternoon tea-break to top up your fruit and veg quota for the day and keep your energy levels in tip-top condition.

sweet treats and savoury bites

The following ideas are all designed to boost your fruit intake. For variety, alternate between these and the dips (see page 127).

Eat whole fruits and keep it varied to avoid boredom. Go for apricots, peaches, nectarines, plums, kiwis, crisp apples, bananas, pears, satsumas or clementines, strawberries, grapes or cherries.

Prepare a tub of fruits for that mid-morning munchy moment: add chunks of fresh pineapple, cubes of mango, slices of paw paw, two types of melon cubes or fresh fruit salad. For sweet treat variety add a pot of Bio or Greek yogurt and some runny honey.

Simple avocado: serve halved ripe avocado, plain and simple, with some vinaigrette in the centre or just with a wedge of lemon and olive oil, salt and a pepper grinder on the table.

Minty grapefruit: allow one grapefruit per person, halve and cut out the flesh. Remove the white skin. Mix the flesh with chopped fresh mint and sugar or honey to taste, then pile back into the skin to serve.

Melon moments: dice wedges of melon or scoop into balls with a melon-baller. Using two melons with different coloured flesh mixed together makes an attractive colourful combination.

Lettuce play: spoon good quality bought hummus on top of crunchy shredded little gem or iceberg lettuce and grated carrot, topped with some black olives and serve with a wedge of lemon

Garlic mushrooms: halve firm white mushrooms, fry in butter, olive oil or a mixture with crushed garlic. Allow 125 g/4 oz mushrooms and 1 fat garlic clove per person and serve with lots of good bread to mop up the juices

Awesome asparagus: cook asparagus in boiling water until it's tender enough to get the point of a knife through – 4–7 minutes, depending on the thickness. Drain and serve with melted butter, olive oil and lemon wedges or vinaigrette.

Butter broccoli: cook purple sprouting broccoli and serve in a pool of salty butter. It's so good it's like the winter version of asparagus and can be served in the same ways.

Nice but naughty snack ideas on the calorie-content front include home-made fruit cake, apple cake or date slices (see lunch and supper puddings).

Mixes of nuts, seeds and assorted dried fruits make great snacking material. Use raisins, sultanas, dried cherries, apricots or dates but remember to keep them fresh in a lidded container or twist of foil.

You don't have to wait until Christmas to enjoy really fab and very more-ish combos, such as plump, juicy ready-to-eat prunes each stuffed with a brazil nut; or fresh or dried dates stuffed with almonds.

dips and dippers

Dunking crisp veg into creamy dips is very more-ish and children love them. Here are a few suggestions for mouth-watering dips that can be used as snacks or even starters at a leisurely meal.

Crudités: use any raw veg you fancy. It sometimes pays to get ready-prepared veg from the supermarket if you're short of time. Any of the following can be used for dunking:

radishes
sticks of cucumber
sticks of carrot
sticks of red or golden pepper
sticks of celery
spring onions
halved cherry tomatoes
mangetout peas
florets of cauliflower or broccoli (these make the best dippers of all)

Serve with your favourite dip, bought or home-made. For example:

Hummus: buy or make this by putting a drained can of chick peas, 2 or more crushed garlic cloves, 4 tablespoons tahini and 100 ml/3 fl oz fresh lemon juice into a food processor and whizzing to a creamy purée.

Tsatsiki: stir peeled and finely cubed cucumber into thick Bio or Greek yogurt with a little crushed garlic, chopped mint and spring onion; season with salt and pepper.

Lite avocado: roughly mash a small avocado and mix with 2 chopped tomatoes, 4 chopped spring onions, 4 heaped tablespoons fromage frais, a crushed garlic clove and 2 tablespoons chopped fresh coriander. Flavour with a dash of tabasco or chilli powder and season with salt and pepper.

Green goddess: thaw 225 g/8 oz of frozen chopped spinach then press in a sieve to get it as dry as you can. Mix the spinach with 4 tablespoons of mayonnaise, 100 g crème fraîche and salt and pepper for a very yummy dip.

Chilli cannellini: whiz 2 garlic cloves in a food processor to chop, then add a drained can of cannellini beans, the juice of 1 lemon and some pepper and whiz to a cream. Put into a bowl then add a teaspoonful or fresh red chilli from a jar or sambal oelek, which you can get from large supermarkets, and stir it through the dip to fleck it with red.

Dunking crisp veg into creamy dips is very more-ish – children love eating vegetables like this

nutty pepper dip

Brick-red and fab, worth the effort of making it. You can get jars of red chilli at supermarkets or use sambal oelek, which is also available at large supermarkets.

25 g/1 oz almonds
2 large red peppers
slice of bread, white or brown
1 tablespoon olive oil
2 garlic cloves
$^1/_2$–1 teaspoon 'fresh red chilli' (from a jar) or sambal oelek
1 teaspoon balsamic vinegar

Skin the almonds by putting them into a small pan, covering them with cold water, bringing to the boil and simmering for 1 minute.

Drain and slip off the skins, then toast the almonds under the grill until they're golden brown but watch them as they only take a minute or two.

Halve and deseed 2 red peppers and grill until they're tender and flecked with black. Cool slightly and skin them if preferred.

Fry the bread in the olive oil. Put the nuts into a food processor with the garlic and whiz until quite fine, then put in all the remaining ingredients and whiz to a thick brick-red dip.

Season with salt and pepper.

Servings 2–4 Fruit/veg portions 4

sauce and spice

Sweet and savoury sauces are a fabulous accompaniment to many fruit and veg dishes and can be kept in the fridge or frozen to accompany a main meal or snack. Here are some saucy ideas that you can take out and use at any time of day or night!

raspberry revival

You can make a blackberry sauce in exactly the same way – either tastes marvellous with cooked apple purée or chopped sweet raw apple. Both the sauces freeze well.

450 g/1 lb fresh or frozen raspberries
2–3 tablespoons caster sugar
1–2 tablespoons of water

Purée the raspberries in a food processor, then push them through a sieve to remove the seeds.

Sweeten the resulting sauce with 2–3 tablespoons of caster sugar to taste and add a tablespoonful or so of water to thin it a little if necessary.

Serves 4 Fruit/veg portions 5–6

wicked chocolate

This sauce is very easy to make and has a deep, dark flavour.
Add a bit more cream if you find it too intense. If you can get real
Madagascar Bourbon vanilla extract, available from specialty stores
and some major supermarkets, it tastes fabulous.

4 tablespoons cocoa powder
4 tablespoons caster sugar
150 ml/5 fl oz water
15 g/¹/₂ oz butter
2 tablespoons single cream
1 teaspoon vanilla extract

Put the cocoa powder and sugar into a saucepan. Add a little of
the water and blend to a smooth paste, then stir in the rest.

Set the pan over a gentle heat and bring to the boil, stirring often.
This mixture burns easily so take care. Remove from the heat and
stir in the butter, cream and vanilla.

Serve hot or cold. The sauce will thicken as it cools.

Serves 4 Fruit/vegetable portions 0

a touch of the tropics

This is fab with tropical fruit – chunks of pineapple, mango, banana, pawpaw and persimmon. For a variation, scoop out the pulp from a passion fruit and stir that into the dip before serving. Alternatively use the dip as a topping for exotic fruit salad

200 g/7 oz block of creamed coconut
juice and grated rind of 1 lime
4 tablespoons boiling water
225 g–450 g/8 oz–1 lb tropical fruit chunks

Cut the creamed coconut into pieces, put into a china or glass bowl or serving dish and melt in the microwave; or set the bowl over a pan of boiling water until the coconut has melted.

Remove from the heat and gently stir in the lime juice and rind and enough boiling water to make the mixture as soft as you want – it will firm up a bit as it cools.

Put the fruit into another bowl and serve with the dip.

Serves 2–4 Fruit/veg portions 2–3

appley-dappley

Apple sauce is a delicious way of adding extra fruit to a meal.
It's very quick and easy to make, particularly if you use a microwave.

500 g/1 lb sweet or cooking apples, peeled and sliced
caster sugar

Put the apples in a shallow dish suitable for the microwave, or in a
saucepan if you're using the stove.

Add 2 tablespoons of water. Cover and microwave or simmer for 10
minutes or until tender. Stir in a little sugar to taste.

Servings 4 Fruit/veg portions 4

tangy red onion marmalade

This sweet, tangy red conserve goes well with many savoury dishes and appeals to people who aren't keen on vegetables. It keeps well for several weeks in the refrigerator.

1 kg/2 lb red onions
2 tablespoons olive oil
salt
2 tablespoons sugar
3 tablespoons sherry
2 tablespoons red wine vinegar
freshly ground black pepper

Peel the onions, cut them in half and slice thinly to make half moons.

Heat the oil in a large saucepan, stir in the onions and allow them to cook gently for 5 minutes. Add some salt, then cover and cook for a further 10 minutes until they are very tender (the onions must be really soft).

Add the the sugar, sherry and vinegar and cook gently over low heat, uncovered, stirring occasionally, for about 30 minutes, or until the mixture is thick and sticky with hardly any liquid left.

Remove from the heat, season with more salt if needed and a grinding of pepper.

Servings 8 (about 650 ml/1 pint) Fruit/veg portions 10–12

sweetcorn relish

This gorgeous relish is an easy way to eat a good portion of vegetables and is something that children like, particularly if served with meat or veggie burgers. They may prefer a little less onion in the mixture, or none at all, and the recipe can be adapted to taste. Fresh, frozen or canned sweetcorn are all suitable for this recipe. If you're using canned, look for the kind without added salt or sugar.

1 red pepper, deseeded and chopped
1 medium onion, peeled and finely chopped
250 g/8 oz cooked sweetcorn kernels, cut from the cob or
thawed frozen sweetcorn, or a 340 g/12 oz can sweetcorn, drained
juice of 1 lime
4 tablespoons coriander, chopped
good pinch of chilli powder
salt and freshly ground black pepper

Put the pepper, onion and sweetcorn into a large bowl. Add the lime juice and coriander and mix together.

Add chilli powder to your taste and season with salt and pepper. If possible, leave for 1 hour or so before using to allow the flavours to develop.

Servings 4 Fruit/veg portions 6

versatile vinaigrette

Vary this dressing by using red wine vinegar, rice vinegar and freshly squeezed lemon juice instead of balsamic vinegar, or by adding a teaspoonful or so of Dijon mustard or a little crushed garlic. For a lighter dressing, use a mixture of vinegar and lemon juice and reduce the amount of oil.

6 tablespoons olive oil
2 tablespoons balsamic vinegar
1 teaspoon sea salt
freshly ground black pepper

Put the ingredients in a clean screw-top jar and shake to combine well. Keep in a cool place and use as desired.

Makes 125 ml/4 fl oz Fruit/veg portions 0

Make a simple dressing right over a served salad with a squeeze of fresh lemon juice, a splash of vinegar, a drizzle of olive oil, and a sprinkle of salt and black pepper

real-time coleslaw

It's worth making coleslaw yourself, as it's really quick and easy, and will keep in the fridge, if well covered, for several days. For a change, or to make a more subtantial dish, you can include all sorts of additional ingredients for almost endless variations.

250 g/8 oz firm green cabbage, such as sweetheart
2 or 3 carrots, scraped or peeled
6 spring onions, chopped
2 heaped tablespoons thick yogurt
2 heaped tablespoons mayonnaise
salt and freshly ground black pepper
fresh lemon juice

Halve or quarter the cabbage and remove the central core. Cut it into thin shreds with a sharp knife and put into a bowl.

Grate the carrots into the bowl and add the spring onion along with the yogurt, mayonnaise and seasoning. Stir to mix well. Taste and add lemon juice and adjust the seasoning if necessary.

Servings 2–4 Fruit/veg portions 4

Variation: For a dressier version, mix in one, two or several of the following additions shortly before serving: grapes, pineapple cubes, chopped apple, chopped red pepper, chopped tomato, diced celery, snipped dried apricots, raisins or sultanas, cubed or grated cheese or cooked small prawns.

tomato treat

A home-made tomato sauce can be a tasty and effective way of adding an extra portion of vegetables to a meal, and it couldn't be easier to make. It freezes well too.

1 tablespoon olive oil
1 onion, peeled and chopped
1 garlic clove, crushed
425 g/15 oz can chopped tomatoes in juice
salt and freshly ground black pepper

Heat the oil in a medium-sized saucepan and stir in the onion. Cover and cook gently for 7 minutes or until the onion has softened.

Add the garlic and tomatoes and cook, uncovered, for 15–20 minutes, stirring occasionally, until the sauce has thickened. Season with salt and pepper.

Serve it chunky or, if you like it smooth, purée using a blender or food processor.

Servings 2 Fruit/veg portions 4

Variation: To vary the basic sauce, add a teaspoonful of dried thyme or oregano with the garlic, a spoonful of sun-dried tomato paste, a splash of wine or finish off with a tablespoonful or so of cream.

japanese dipping sauce

You can buy Japanese horseradish – wasabi – in powdered form to mix with liquid or ready made in a tube from oriental food shops. If you can't get it, use the same quantity of Dijon mustard instead. Mirin is fortifed rice wine, which you can buy, reasonably priced, from oriental food shops and specialist grocers. It is also very useful for adding a sweet flavour to stir-fries.

2 tablespoons soy sauce
2 tablespoons mirin or sherry
1/4–1/2 teaspoon wasabi powder or paste
1/2 teaspoon toasted sesame seeds

Stir together the soy sauce, mirin and wasabi; start with the smaller quantity of wasabi (or mustard) and add more to taste, because it's quite hot.

Put the dip into a small bowl or individual bowls and sprinkle the sesame seeds over the top. Serve with vegetable tempura.

Servings 2 Fruit/veg portions 0

index